Bible Encounter Series
SEEING JESUS
Workbook

VOLUME 2 HISTORY
JOSHUA to ESTHER

Marilyn Hickey

Marilyn & Sarah

marilynandsarah.org

Marilyn Hickey Ministries • 8081 East Orchard Road, Suite 135 • Greenwood Village, CO 80111-2675

Unless otherwise indicated, all Scriptures quoted in this volume are from the New Internatonal Version of the Bible.

BIBLE ENCOUNTER SERIES
SEEING JESUS WORKBOOK, VOLUME 2

2014
by Marilyn Hickey Ministries

marilynandsarah.org

All rights reserved

PRODUCT CODE: SJWB2

Printed in the United States of America

ISBN # 978-1-938696-73-2

CONTENTS

Introduction	4		Lesson 12 - 2 Kings: God's Records	60
Joshua DVD 1 Lesson	6		Lesson 13 - 1 Chronicles: Reviewing David's Kingdom	64
Lesson 6 - Joshua: Victory	8		Kings & Prophets 3 DVD 2 Lesson	70
Judges & Ruth DVD 1 Lesson	14		Lesson 14 - 2 Chronicles: Reviewing David's Kingdom	74
Lesson 7 - Judges: Righteous Judge	18		Ezra, Nehemiah, and Esther DVD 2 Lesson	80
Lesson 8 - Ruth: Kinsman Redeemer	24		Lesson 15 - Ezra: Faithful Scribe	84
1 & 2 Samuel DVD 1 Lesson	30		Lesson 16 - Nehemiah: Restorer & Rebuilder	90
Lesson 9 - 1 Samuel: The Prophet	34		Lesson 17 - Esther: Intercessor	96
Lesson 10 - 2 Samuel: The Deliverer	40		Appendex	105
Kings & Prophets 1 DVD 2 Lesson	46		Leader's Guide	107
Lesson 11 - 1 Kings: God's Records	50		Additional Study Notes	111
Kings & Prophets 2 DVD 2 Lesson	56		Answer Key	117

INTRODUCTION

I love Jesus.

When you receive Him into your heart, it's totally transformational. I was 16 years-old when I got born again. I was raised in a somewhat liberal church so I knew about Him but I didn't know I could have Him. Later I went to a youth camp and I learned that you could have Jesus inside—Christ in you, the hope of glory. So I prayed, repented of my sins, and invited him to come into my heart and be Lord of my life. And from 16 years-old to now I can say He has never left me or forsaken me and He is real and He can be real in your life every day.

But, I wondered, how can you see who He really is? So I began to read the Bible and I found that Jesus is in every book of the Bible. This knowledge sparked such a passion in me to get everyone hooked on the whole book—to see him in Genesis all the way through to Revelation. Often we say, "Who is Jesus in the Old Testament?" But He is in every book!

I wanted to get people to see who Jesus is inside them—how the Bible reveals who He is in each book inside them. So I began with home Bible studies. I love home Bible studies to this day. So even now I'm doing a home Bible study with you in your home straight from my home.

Many times we don't read the Old Testament. We say it's so confusing but it's not once you see who Jesus is in you in the Old Testament. When you look at the Old Testament you will see that it divides into five segments. So if we know where we are going, we'll know when we get there. It's the transformation of Jesus in your life.

We will be looking at and we will see Jesus in the Pentateuch, in the History books, the Poetry and Wisdom books, the Major and Minor Prophets, and the Gospels, Acts and Romans, the Letters and the End Times.

The *Seeing Jesus Bible Encounter* is a foundational, cornerstone teaching which came from years of in-depth, spirit-guided study of the Word.

My prayer is that your relationship with our Savior Jesus Christ will be deeper and more precious after you dig in and see Jesus in every book of the Bible.

His Love and Mine,

Marilyn Hickey

JOSHUA: VICTORY
VIDEO SEGMENT LESSON GUIDE

INTRODUCTION TO *SEEING JESUS* (10-15 MINUTES):

Joshua is usually a favorite character in the Bible. He was a man with great courage to carry out God's plan for the Israelites to enter the Promised Land. His name is the Old Testament equivalent to the name, "Jesus." Names in the Bible were always very important. Do you have a namesake? Share family history of your name or someone you may know who was named after a relative.

Watch video segment (approx. 20-30 minutes). Take notes and fill in the blanks.

Brief overview:

1. Joshua is the first of the _____ books.
2. After they cross the Jordan River, the _____ will stop.
3. They are going take the Promised Land in _____ years.
4. Do not let this Book of the Law depart from your mouth; _____ on it day and night, so that you may be careful to do everything written in it. Joshua 1:8
5. Joshua was in charge of about _____ people.

Jericho/instructions (Joshua 5-6):

Rahab:

Crossing the Jordan (Joshua 3):

> " *THE WORD MAKES YOU* **HEALTHY AND SUCCESSFUL.** "

The priests take the ark of the covenant through the water.

Jesus sighting:
The Word took them through!
Jesus covered all of our sin, all the way back to Adam.

Gibeonites:

Greatest faith statement in the Bible: "Sun, stand still..." (Joshua 10:12).

Jesus Sightings in Joshua (15 minutes):
Take a look at the battle of Jericho in chapter 6. Reference your notes as well from the video and discuss the instructions God gave Joshua to overtake the city.

> " *AS FOR ME AND MY HOUSE, WE WILL* **SERVE THE LORD.** "

What divine intervention can we see that goes well beyond Joshua's abilities?

What is your Jericho you are facing? What divine intervention are you asking for to have victory?

Joshua also led God's people through the Jordan River. What similarities do you see in this miracle as with Moses and the Red Sea?

Wrap Up (10-15 minutes):
Marilyn challenged participants to pick a chapter in the Bible to memorize. What comes to mind? Write down some steps that will enable you to stick to this goal.

Spend time sharing prayer requests and closing in prayer. Thank Jesus for covering our sin with His victory!

JOSHUA: VICTORY

In your SEEING JESUS Study Guide:
Read through the fast facts, author and setting, and overview on page 69 and 70. Reflect and take notes.

Jesus in Joshua:

The name Joshua is the Old Testament equivalent for Yeshua, Jesus, which means "Yahweh Saves!" As we study this book, we can see that the life of Joshua was another "type" of Jesus. His name is appropriately chosen to lead the Israelites into the Promised Land. The author shows that God has been faithful to fulfill His promise to Abraham to give his descendants the land of Canaan and that He would bless obedience to the covenant relationship.

Read Joshua 2:1-24.
Circle or underline all that is significant about Rahab:

Rahab and the Spies:
Then Joshua son of Nun secretly sent two spies from Shittim. "Go, look over the land," he said, "especially Jericho." So they went and entered the house of a prostitute named Rahab and stayed there.

2 The king of Jericho was told, "Look, some of the Israelites have come here tonight to spy out the land." **3** So the king of Jericho sent this message to Rahab: "Bring out the men who came to you and entered your house, because they have come to spy out the whole land."

4 But the woman had taken the two men and hidden them. She said, "Yes, the men came to me, but I did not know where they had come from. **5** At dusk, when it was time to close the city gate, they left. I don't know which way they went. Go after them quickly. You may catch up with them." **6** (But she had taken them up to the roof and hidden them under the stalks of flax she had laid out on the roof.) **7** So the men set out in pursuit of the spies on the road that leads to the fords of the Jordan, and as soon as the pursuers had gone out, the gate was shut.

8 Before the spies lay down for the night, she went up on the roof **9** and said to them, "I know that the Lord has given you this land and that a great fear of you has fallen on us, so that all who live in this country are melting in fear because of you. **10** We have heard how the Lord dried up the water of the Red Sea for you when you came out of Egypt, and what you did to Sihon and Og, the two kings of the Amorites east of the Jordan, whom you completely destroyed. **11** When we heard of it, our hearts melted in fear and everyone's courage failed because of you, for the Lord your God is God in heaven above and on the earth below.

12 "Now then, please swear to me by the Lord that you will show kindness to my family, because I have shown kindness to you. Give me a sure sign **13** that you will spare the lives of my father and mother, my brothers and sisters, and all who belong to them, and that you will save us from death." **14** "Our lives for your lives!" the men assured her. "If you don't tell what we are doing, we will treat you kindly and faithfully when the Lord gives us the land."

15 So she let them down by a rope through the window, for the house she lived in was part of the city wall. **16** She said to them, "Go to the hills so the pursuers will not find you. Hide yourselves there three days until they return, and then go on your way."

17 Now the men had said to her, "This oath you made us swear will not be binding on us **18** unless, when we enter the land, you have tied this scarlet cord in the window through which you let us down, and unless you have brought your father and mother, your brothers and all your family into your house. **19** If any of them go outside your house into the street, their blood will be on their own heads; we will not be responsible. As for those who are in the house with you, their blood will be on our head if a hand is laid on them. **20** But if you tell what we are doing, we will be released from the oath you made us swear."

21 "Agreed," she replied. "Let it be as you say."
So she sent them away, and they departed. And she tied the scarlet cord in the window.

22 When they left, they went into the hills and stayed there three days, until the pursuers had searched all along the road and returned without finding them. **23** Then the two men started back. They went down out of the hills, forded the river and came to Joshua son of Nun and told him everything that had happened to them. **24** They said to Joshua, "The Lord has surely given the whole land into our hands; all the people are melting in fear because of us."

Reflection Exercises:
Write a short paragraph describing who Rahab was and what she did.

_____
_____
_____
_____
_____
_____

Through Rahab, how do we see a glimpse of the grace of Jesus at work?

Re-read Joshua 2:8-11. What does Rahab confess to the spies?

Rahab is mentioned in two significant places in the New Testament; in the genealogy of Jesus and in Hebrews 11, the Hall of Faith. Read Matthew 1:5 and Hebrews 11:31. How do we see Rahab as a recipient of grace, even before the Cross?

> *I KNOW THAT THE LORD HAS GIVEN YOU THIS LAND AND THAT A GREAT FEAR OF YOU HAS FALLEN ON US, SO THAT ALL WHO LIVE IN THIS COUNTRY ARE MELTING IN FEAR BECAUSE OF YOU.* — **JOSHUA 2:9**

 **Unpacking the Outline:**
See the lesson outline for Joshua on page 71 and 72 of your *Seeing Jesus Study Guide*

Spiritual Preparation of Joshua:

Read Joshua 5:13-15.

    What did Joshua see?

    What did the "drawn sword" symbolize for Joshua?

    What was asked of Joshua?

    What was Joshua's response?

The purpose of Joshua's encounter was to inspire humility and reverence and to instill in him the confidence that God was with him and was in control.

Focus: Central Verse / Passage
Joshua 1:8

Keep this Book of the Law always on your lips; meditate on it day and night, so that you may be careful to do everything written in it. Then you will be prosperous and successful.

> HERE THE LAW IS RE-EMPHASIZED TO JOSHUA AS THEY ARE ABOUT TO CROSS OVER INTO THE PROMISED LAND. THE PHRASE **"ON YOUR LIPS"** MEANS TO LITERALLY MUTTER, TO ALWAYS HAVE IT IN THOUGHT.

Write down the practical protection that comes from observing the Ten Commandments? How are we protected through these boundaries?

_____
_____
_____
_____
_____

Throughout the book of Joshua we can see:

1. God is the God of Israel (Joshua 1)
2. God is holy (Joshua 7)
3. God is gracious (e.g., Rahab Joshua 2, the Gibeonites Joshua 11)
4. God is the God of Creation (Joshua 10:9-14; sun stands still)
5. God is a God of the entire universe; all people (Joshua 2:11)
6. God is a man of war (Joshua 5; gave battle strategies to Israelites)

Memory Verse for Lesson:
Have I not commanded you? Be strong and of good courage; do not be afraid, nor be dismayed, for the Lord your God is with you wherever you go (Joshua 1:9 NKJV).

THE ?ARADOXICAL JESUS in JOSHUA

We know the Bible does not contradict itself, so it is important we take time to study and understand all sides of the truth and interpret Scripture in light of Scripture to understand.

Think about it:
We see the grace of God swell up in the story of Rahab and her willingness to believe in the God of Israel and abandon her Canaanite gods. However, a struggle arises as we see in Joshua the extermination of the Canaanites. Men, women, and children were included in this.

How can we walk alongside God's grace and accept when God moves to wipe out a people group?

_____
_____
_____
_____
_____

What might be a modern day example of this tension?

_____
_____
_____
_____
_____

The Canaanites illustrate to us that evil is real and the Devil exists. This struggle took Jesus to the Cross.

I saw Jesus more clearly in this book when...

_____
_____
_____
_____

JESUS UP CLOSE:

JUDGES & RUTH
VIDEO SEGMENT LESSON GUIDE

INTRODUCTION TO *SEEING JESUS* (10-15 MINUTES):
This study is all about seeing Jesus throughout the Bible. As we begin lesson 7, think about ways the Lord is showing you Jesus in your daily life more clearly since you started on this journey in the Word.

Watch video segment (Approx. 20-30 minutes). Take notes and fill in the blanks.

1. We see Jesus in the power of the _____ in the history of the Judges.

2. There are five judges who were _____ .

3. This is the generation that did not experience the _____ in Moses' day.

JUDGES:

Othniel -

Barak and Deborah -

4. "The _____ carried her."

Judges 5: God moved the stars and it began to rain.

Jael -

Gideon -

> *GIDEON, YOU MIGHTY MAN OF VALOR.* **YOU WILL DRIVE OUT THE MIDIANITES.**

The Midianites came in as the enemy and were very cruel, worshippers of Baal.
God raises up Gideon to confront them.

5. "God _____ us in the power of the Holy Spirit."

Through the story of Gideon, we see for the first time the revelation of peace.

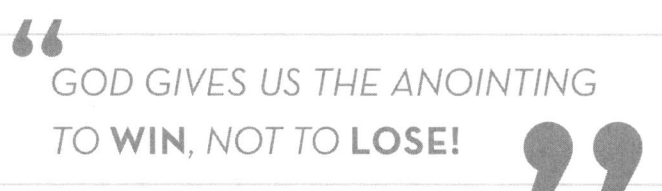

Jephthah –

6. The enemy defeated through Jephthah were the _____ .

Samson –

7. Samson is known for acts of _____ .

He killed more people in his death than in his life.

BOOK OF RUTH:

Ruth –

8. We can do the _____ , the _____ , or the _____ .

Boaz/kinsman redeemer

" WHEN YOU WALK IN **FAITH**, GOD HAS THE **EXTRAORDINARY** FOR YOU! "

God used Naomi to progress the geneology of the Messiah. Her life was a link between Abraham and King David.

NAOMI — HAS A GRANDSON… — OBED — HAS A SON… — JESSE — DAVID

15

Jesus Sightings in Judges/Ruth (15 minutes):

Judges is a book that shows the struggles of falling away in disobedience. Though God used these judges to defeat the enemy, God's people would lapse back into forgetting their God and following idolatry. What are some conscious ways we can carry on our faith to our children and their children?

___
___
___
___

What was one of the main ways we see Jesus manifesting throughout the book according to the video segment?

___
___
___
___

Gideon is a great example of how God uses us in our weaknesses. Think about your last trial and the weakness you had that intimidated you. How did God's strength pull you through?

___
___
___
___

Wrap Up (10-15 minutes):

In looking at the story of Ruth, we can choose to do: the expected, the exception, or the extraordinary. Share a time when you had to step out in faith like Ruth and follow God, though it meant doing the unexpected.

Spend time sharing prayer requests and closing in prayer.

LESSON 7

JUDGES: RIGHTEOUS JUDGE

In your SEEING JESUS Study Guide:
Read through the fast facts, author and setting, and overview on page 75 and 76. Reflect and take notes.

Jesus in Judges:

This book records the story of Israel from the death of Joshua to Samuel. A judge was viewed as a type of savior or ruler, both a spiritual guide and political deliverer. There were fifteen judges, a cumulative picture of Jesus as the ultimate prophet, priest, and king.

Gideon: God chose Gideon to free the Israelites from the Midianites. Once again, God's people turned away from Him, though He warned them to not forget Him. The Lord chose Him, to free God's people.

Read Judges 6:11-29.
Circle words or phrases about Gideon that reflect the image of Jesus.

The angel of the Lord came and sat down under the oak in Ophrah that belonged to Joash the Abiezrite, where his son Gideon was threshing wheat in a winepress to keep it from the Midianites. **12** When the angel of the Lord appeared to Gideon, he said, "The Lord is with you, mighty warrior."
13 "Pardon me, my lord," Gideon replied, "but if the Lord is with us, why has all this happened to us? Where are all his wonders that our ancestors told us about when they said, 'Did not the Lord bring us up out of Egypt?' But now the Lord has abandoned us and given us into the hand of Midian."

> "...GO IN THE STRENGTH YOU HAVE AND SAVE ISRAEL OUT OF MIDIAN'S HAND. AM I NOT SENDING YOU?"
> — JUDGES 6:14

14 The Lord turned to him and said, "Go in the strength you have and save Israel out of Midian's hand. Am I not sending you?"
15 "Pardon me, my lord," Gideon replied, "but how can I save Israel? My clan is the weakest in Manasseh, and I am the least in my family."
16 The Lord answered, "I will be with you, and you will strike down all the Midianites leaving none alive." **17** Gideon replied, "If now I have found favor in your eyes, give me a sign that it is really you talking to me. **18** Please do not go away until I come back and bring my offering and set it before you." And the Lord said, "I will wait until you return."

19 Gideon went inside, prepared a young goat, and from an ephah of flour he made bread without yeast. Putting the meat in a basket and its broth in a pot, he brought them out and offered them to him under the oak. **20** The angel of God said to him, "Take the meat and the unleavened bread, place them on this rock, and pour out the broth." And Gideon did so. **21** Then the angel of the Lord touched the meat and the unleavened bread with the tip of the staff that was in his hand. Fire flared from the rock, consuming the meat and the bread. And the angel of the Lord disappeared.

22 When Gideon realized that it was the angel of the Lord, he exclaimed, "Alas, Sovereign Lord! I have seen the angel of the Lord face to face!" **23** But the Lord said to him, "Peace! Do not be afraid. You are not going to die." **24** So Gideon built an altar to the Lord there and called it The Lord Is Peace. To this day it stands in Ophrah of the Abiezrites.

25 That same night the Lord said to him, "Take the second bull from your father's herd, the one seven years old. Tear down your father's altar to Baal and cut down the Asherah pole beside it. **26** Then build a proper kind of altar to the Lord your God on the top of this height. Using the wood of the Asherah pole that you cut down, offer the second bull as a burnt offering."

27 So Gideon took ten of his servants and did as the Lord told him. But because he was afraid of his family and the townspeople, he did it at night rather than in the daytime.
28 In the morning when the people of the town got up, there was Baal's altar, demolished, with the Asherah pole beside it cut down and the second bull sacrificed on the newly built altar!
29 They asked each other, "Who did this?"

When they carefully investigated, they were told, "Gideon son of Joash did it."

Reflection Exercises:
Write a short description of Gideon after reading this passage:

_____
_____
_____
_____
_____
_____
_____
_____

The Hebrew indicates that Gideon was clothed in the Spirit. He seemed to have so many holes of unbelief that the Spirit had to clothe him to make him the deliverer that he needed to be.

Gideon's call follows the pattern of others, such as Moses. Ironically, God calls him a "mighty warrior" though Gideon himself was hiding from the enemy. What attributes of God are more clear through Gideon's weaknesses?

_____
_____
_____
_____
_____

Gideon came from a weaker clan and within his family, his position was lowly. According to verse 14, what was Gideon's source of strength?

_____
_____
_____
_____
_____

Before delivering Israel, God asked Gideon to take action within his own family, which is often the hardest thing to do. (Jesus also showed His ultimate loyalty was to His Heavenly Father.) His father was worshipping Baal. What could potentially have happened to Gideon for obeying the Lord?

_____
_____
_____
_____
_____

Unpacking the Outline:
See the lesson outline for Judges on page 77 and 78 of your *Seeing Jesus Study Guide*.

Besides Gideon, there were four other judges who were said to be Spirit-filled. Identify the enemy the Lord raised them up to fight. Describe how the Holy Spirit moved upon these judges in the following verses:

1. Othniel, Judges 3:10: _____

2. Deborah, Judges 4:4: _____

3. Jephthah, Judges 11:29: _____

4. Samson, Judges 13:25, 14:6,19: _____

We hear throughout the book of Judges, "Again the Israelites did evil in the sight of the Lord." Continually, though warned, the Israelites fell into compromise and worshiped other gods. In what ways has God's people followed this pattern of worshiping other gods even today in the church?

_____
_____
_____
_____
_____

🔍 Focus: Central Verse / Passage
Judges 21: 15

"In those days Israel had no king; everyone did as he saw fit"

Not only do we have repeated generations of idol worship, but the book closes with the reality that humanity was living with their own moral standards, not God's.

What can we learn from the patterns set in front of us throughout the rule of the judges?

_____
_____
_____
_____
_____

Only by God's mercy were the Israelites able to survive their association with pagan nations. How did God continually show His pursuit of His people?

Memory verse for lesson:
Then the Israelites did evil in the eyes of the Lord, and served the Baals; 12 They forsook the Lord, the God of their fathers, who had brought them out of Egypt. They followed and worshiped various gods of the peoples around them. They provoked the Lord to anger (Judges 2:11-12 NKJV).

THE ?ARADOXICAL JESUS in JUDGES

We know the Bible does not contradict itself, so it is important we take time to study and understand all sides of the truth and interpret Scripture in light of Scripture to understand.

Reread the following verses:
The tension a reader may have of this book is the apparent approval of the gruesome killings of Ehud (Judges 3:12-30) and Jael (Judges 4:17-24).

How did Ehud and Jael display cruelty to the enemy that seems contradictory to God's nature?

In these examples, did God instruct them to kill in this manner?

Another problem to reconcile is why God chose men who struggled with immorality, like Samson. In God's sovereignty, His Spirit came upon such men with great power. Does this pattern follow into the New Testament examples of men mightily used by God whose behavior is open to serious question?

___

Though humanity continues to be unfaithful, God continues to be faithful.

I saw Jesus more clearly in this book when…

JESUS UP CLOSE:

RUTH: KINSMAN REDEEMER

In your SEEING JESUS Study Guide:
Read through the fast facts, author and setting, and overview on page 83 and 84. Reflect and take notes.

Jesus in Ruth:

The story of Ruth is said to be one of the most beautiful stories written. The authorship is not stated in the book, but Jewish tradition credits Samuel. The story occurs at the time during the Judges. We see Jesus in the man, Boaz, acting as a kinsman-redeemer. Take time to read the entire book of Ruth in one sitting. Summarize the events that happened to Ruth, Naomi, and Boaz.

 DEFINITION OF **"KINSMAN-REDEEMER"**: MALE RELATIVE WHO, ACCORDING TO VARIOUS LAWS FOUND IN THE PENTATEUCH, HAD THE PRIVILEGE OR RESPONSIBILITY TO ACT FOR A RELATIVE WHO WAS IN TROUBLE, DANGER, OR NEED OF VINDICATION.

Now re-read the following passage and circle the ways Boaz cares for Ruth, much like Jesus cares for us.

Ruth 2:1-21

Now Naomi had a relative on her husband's side, a man of standing from the clan of Elimelek, whose name was Boaz.
2 And Ruth the Moabite said to Naomi, "Let me go to the fields and pick up the leftover grain behind anyone in whose eyes I find favor."

Naomi said to her, "Go ahead, my daughter." **3** So she went out, entered a field and began to glean behind the harvesters. As it turned out, she was working in a field belonging to Boaz, who was from the clan of Elimelek.
4 Just then Boaz arrived from Bethlehem and greeted the harvesters, "The Lord be with you!"

"The Lord bless you!" they answered.

5 Boaz asked the overseer of his harvesters, "Who does that young woman belong to?"
6 The overseer replied, "She is the Moabite who came back from Moab with Naomi. **7** She said, 'Please let me glean and gather among the sheaves behind the harvesters.' She came into the field and has remained here from morning till now, except for a short rest in the shelter."

8 So Boaz said to Ruth, "My daughter, listen to me. Don't go and glean in another field and don't go away from here. Stay here with the women who work for me. **9** Watch the field where the men are harvesting, and follow along after the women. I have told the men not to lay a hand on you. And whenever you are thirsty, go and get a drink from the water jars the men have filled."

10 At this, she bowed down with her face to the ground. She asked him, "Why have I found such favor in your eyes that you notice me—a foreigner?" **11** Boaz replied, "I've been told all about what you have done for your mother-in-law since the death of your husband—how you left your father and mother and your homeland and came to live with a people you did not know before. **12** May the Lord repay you for what you have done. May you be richly rewarded by the Lord, the God of Israel, under whose wings you have come to take refuge." **13** "May I continue to find favor in your eyes, my lord," she said. "You have put me at ease by speaking kindly to your servant—though I do not have the standing of one of your servant."

14 At mealtime Boaz said to her, "Come over here. Have some bread and dip it in the wine vinegar." When she sat down with the harvesters, he offered her some roasted grain. She ate all she wanted and had some left over. **15** As she got up to glean, Boaz gave orders to his men, "Let her gather among the sheaves and don't reprimand her. **16** Even pull out some stalks for her from the bundles and leave them for her to pick up, and don't rebuke her."
17 So Ruth gleaned in the field until evening. Then she threshed the barley she had gathered, and it amounted to about an ephah. **18** She carried it back to town, and her mother-in-law saw how much she had gathered. Ruth also brought out and gave her what she had left over after she had eaten enough.

19 Her mother-in-law asked her, "Where did you glean today? Where did you work? Blessed be the man who took notice of you!" Then Ruth told her mother-in-law about the one at whose place she had been working. "The name of the man I worked with today is Boaz," she said.

20 "The Lord bless him!" Naomi said to her daughter-in-law. "He has not stopped showing his kindness to the living and the dead." She added, "That man is our close relative; he is one of our guardian-redeemers." **21** Then Ruth the Moabite said, "He even said to me, 'Stay with my workers until they finish harvesting all my grain.'"

A kinsman-redeemer must:

1. Be related by blood to those he redeems
2. Be able to pay the redemption
3. Be willing to redeem
4. Be free himself

Reflection Exercises:

How did Boaz greet the harvesters?

What instructions did Boaz give to Ruth?

In what ways did Boaz provide vindication for Ruth and Naomi?

How did this impact Naomi's situation?

How is Jesus a type of kinsman-redeemer to us today?

Unpacking the Outline:
See the lesson outline for Ruth on page 85 and 86 of your *Seeing Jesus Study Guide*

There were seven steps necessary for kinsman redemption to happen. Read over the following:

1. Eyewitness (Ruth 4:2)
2. Agreement (Ruth 4:3-6)
3. Giving up of rights (Ruth 4:7,8)
4. Redemption of the inheritance (Ruth 4:9)
5. Marriage (Ruth 4:10)
6. Confession of transaction (Ruth 4:11)
7. Blessing over marriage (Ruth 4:11)

From Ruth claiming her redemption, God uses family, man's seed, to provide the genealogy of Jesus Christ.

Who was Obed's grandfather?

_____
_____

Who was Boaz' mother?

_____
_____

How do we see God's gift of grace in the redemption of this family line?

_____
_____
_____
_____
_____

The story of Ruth deals beautifully with a close up look at the troubles of a single family in Bethlehem. Through the story of Ruth, we see the concept of divine providence unfold!

Focus: Central Verse / Passage
Ruth 2:12

"May the Lord repay you for what you have done. May you be richly rewarded by the Lord, the God of Israel, under whose wings you have come to take refuge".

Boaz prays a beautiful blessing over Ruth for her decision to follow the God of Israel. She no longer worships the idol Chemosh. But she is recognized as a true worshiper of the Lord.

Memory Verse for Lesson:

Entreat me not to leave you, or to turn back from following after you; For wherever you go, I will go; And wherever you lodge, I will lodge; Your people shall be my people, And your God, my God (Ruth 1:16 NKJV).

THE ?ARADOXICAL JESUS in RUTH

We know the Bible does not contradict itself, so it is important we take time to study and understand all sides of the truth and interpret Scripture in light of Scripture to understand.

Go back and read Ruth, chapter 1.

In all her losses, Naomi also loses hope in God. She tells Ruth on the way to Bethlehem, "Call me Mara, because the Almighty has made my life very bitter." Though originally a Moabite, Ruth is the one to save her mother-in-law by believing in Naomi's God.

God often uses even an ungodly heritage to bring about redemption to a family. How might this be true as you look at your family's spiritual heritage?

_____
_____
_____
_____

How did Ruth's obedience lead to restoring faith in the Almighty?

_____
_____

I saw Jesus more clearly in this book when...

JESUS UP CLOSE:

1 & 2 SAMUEL
VIDEO SEGMENT LESSON GUIDE

INTRODUCTION TO *SEEING JESUS* (10-15 MINUTES):
This study is all about seeing Jesus throughout the Bible. As we begin video lesson 8, think about qualities that reflect godly leadership. What happens to a people when ungodly kings rule? Discuss.

Watch video segment (Approx. 20-30 minutes): Take notes and fill in the blanks.

1. _____ is revealed magnificently in the history books of the Bible!
2. Hannah is a woman very upset and she cannot _____ .
3. Hannah's name means "_____ ."
4. God will use a _____ to bring us a miracle.
5. God doesn't use perfect people because of His _____ .

SAMUEL MEANS: **"ASKED OF GOD."**

Hannah's vow –

Hannah's song –

Hannah is the first one to sing about the Messiah!

When Samuel reaches a certain age, Hannah takes him to the priest and she gives him to the Lord as she promised.

We need to entrust God with our children.

After Samuel, Hannah has five more children. You cannot out-give God!

Samuel sleeps by the Ark of the Covenant (the Word of God!)

Samuel's call from God:

We learn to hear the voice of God.

"Speak Lord, your servant hears."

Samuel becomes the prophet of Israel.

Samuel also received the revelation of the Messiah, just like His mother.

The people don't just want a prophet, but they want a king, and Samuel waits on God.

First King:

Saul, wealthy, tall, handsome comes to Samuel and he is anointed.

Saul continued to disobey God.

Quick Application:

Check your motives when you pray. Work with God in what He wants, not what you want.

David and Goliath:

David is anointed by Samuel.

Saul begins to plot to kill David. In nine years, Saul tried to kill David nineteen times.

David's army begins to grow. David had two opportunities to kill Saul, but he forebears.

David wrote the 23rd Psalm before he went out to fight Goliath.

David becomes a king for forty years. The anointing of God was upon his life.

Christians are "anointed ones."

Psalm 51 – forgiveness is there for the anointed one, Christians.

Jesus Sightings in 1 Samuel (15 minutes):

What a miracle to see Jesus in Hannah's prayer in 1 Samuel 2. Later Samuel has the same revelation from God. God uses the Body to confirm and test truth. How has God confirmed a word He gave you in a recent situation?

_____
_____
_____
_____

Samuel learned to hear the voice of God. Discuss if you grew up believing God speaks today or if he only speaks through the Bible. Share your insights and what you've come to believe about the way God speaks to you:

_____
_____
_____
_____

Marilyn gives the charge to check our motives when we pray. The Bible says to ask, seek, and knock (Matthew 7:7), and He will answer. Sometimes the reason He doesn't answer is because we are not including Him to help shape our requests. What are some ways we can check our motives?

_____
_____
_____
_____

Psalm 51 is a powerful glimpse of God's grace on David after his sin with Bathsheba. What were his requests to God? What can we learn about David's understanding of grace in this psalm?

_____
_____
_____
_____

Wrap Up (10-15 minutes):

Marilyn mentions how all Christians are an "anointed one"—thanks to Jesus Christ. And all of us called to a work prepared in advance for us (Ephesians 2:10). Perhaps share an experience where you worked alongside someone and knew they were anointed for a task. What tasks do you believe He is calling you to do that He has especially equipped you to do?

Spend time sharing prayer requests and closing in prayer.

LESSON 9

1 SAMUEL: THE PROPHET

In your SEEING JESUS Study Guide:
Read through the fast facts, author and setting, and overview on page 93 and 94. Reflect and take notes.

Jesus in 1 Samuel:

God uses his leaders in different ways to bring about His plan. He used Samuel to lead His people through the reign of judges and kings. He also paved the way for 500 years of prophets who would boldly speak God's Word.

Read the passage below. Underline the verses where you can "see" Jesus at work in the life of Samuel:

1 Samuel 3 – The Lord Calls Samuel

The boy Samuel ministered before the Lord under Eli. In those days the word of the Lord was rare; there were not many visions.

2 One night Eli, whose eyes were becoming so weak that he could barely see, was lying down in his usual place. **3** The lamp of God had not yet gone out, and Samuel was lying down in the house of the Lord, where the ark of God was. **4** Then the Lord called Samuel.

Samuel answered, "Here I am." 5 And he ran to Eli and said, "Here I am; you called me."
But Eli said, "I did not call; go back and lie down." So he went and lay down.

6 Again the Lord called, "Samuel!" And Samuel got up and went to Eli and said, "Here I am; you called me."

> *...THE LORD CAME AND STOOD THERE, CALLING AS AT THE OTHER TIMES, "SAMUEL! SAMUEL!" THEN SAMUEL SAID, "SPEAK, FOR YOUR SERVANT IS LISTENING.*

"My son," Eli said, "I did not call; go back and lie down." **7** Now Samuel did not yet know the Lord: The word of the Lord had not yet been revealed to him.

8 A third time the LORD called, "Samuel!" And Samuel got up and went to Eli and said, "Here I am; you called me."

Then Eli realized that the Lord was calling the boy. **9** So Eli told Samuel, "Go and lie down, and if he calls you, say, 'Speak, Lord, for your servant is listening.'" So Samuel went and lay down in his place.

10 The Lord came and stood there, calling as at the other times, "Samuel! Samuel!" Then Samuel said, "Speak, for your servant is listening." **11** And the Lord said to Samuel: "See, I am about to do something in Israel that will make the ears of everyone who hears about it tingle. **12** At that time I will carry out against Eli everything I spoke against his family—from beginning to end. **13** For I told him that I would judge his family forever because of the sin he knew about; his sons blasphemed God, and he failed to restrain them. **14** Therefore I swore to the house of Eli, 'The guilt of Eli's house will never be atoned for by sacrifice or offering.'"

15 Samuel lay down until morning and then opened the doors of the house of the Lord. He was afraid to tell Eli the vision, **16** but Eli called him and said, "Samuel, my son." Samuel answered, "Here I am."

17 "What was it he said to you?" Eli asked. "Do not hide it from me. May God deal with you, be it ever so severely, if you hide from me anything he told you." **18** So Samuel told him everything, hiding nothing from him. Then Eli said, "He is the Lord; let him do what is good in his eyes."

19 The Lord was with Samuel as he grew up, and he let none of Samuel's words fall to the ground. **20** And all Israel from Dan to Beersheba recognized that Samuel was attested as a prophet of the Lord. **21** The Lord continued to appear at Shiloh, and there he revealed himself to Samuel through his word.

Reflection Exercises:
Write a paragraph summarizing the ways you see Jesus in the life of Samuel:

_____
_____
_____
_____
_____
_____
_____

Even as a young boy, Samuel was used greatly to prophesy. The first vision he received was a rebuke on Eli's family. How did Samuel prove to be faithful to God and Eli?

_____
_____
_____
_____

Samuel served in his lifetime as a prophet, priest, and type of ruler. Jesus was also a prophet, priest, and king. In verse 20, we see Samuel was recognized as a prophet of the Lord. According to verse 21, how did God reveal and speak to Samuel (see also John 1:1)?

_____
_____
_____
_____

Scripture tells us to always test a prophecy. How did Eli know Samuel had heard from the Lord? Read 1 Samuel 2:27-36 and 3:11-14.

_____
_____
_____
_____

Samuel learned to recognize the voice of God. What are some ways we can train our ears to hear God's call to us?

_____
_____
_____
_____

> *HE WILL GUARD THE FEET OF HIS SAINTS, BUT THE WICKED WILL BE SILENCED IN DARKNESS. IT IS NOT BY STRENGTH THAT ONE PREVAILS.*
> **— 1 SAMUEL 2:9**

🔍 **Unpacking the Outline:**
See the lesson outline for 1 Samuel on page 97 and 98 of your study guide.

Samuel anointed King Saul and King David. **Read 1 Samuel 9:14-17.**

How did Samuel know God chose Saul to be the next king?

___

Where was Saul from and who was he to fight against?

___

Saul's name means **"ASKED OF GOD."**

King Saul is best known for:
- impressive physical appearance
- courage and generosity in his early reign
- losing God's favor for disobedience
- hatred toward David

Read 1 Samuel 9:1-3. How is Saul described?

___

David is anointed. **Read 1 Samuel 16:7-13.**

What did God tell Samuel to look at in verse 7?

___

Was David's anointing a public or private anointing?

___

Compare and contrast the differences in these two kings from the scriptures read.

KING SAUL	KING DAVID
_____	_____
_____	_____
_____	_____
_____	_____
_____	_____

What was David first known as?

_____
_____
_____

DAVID'S NAME MEANS **"BELOVED OF GOD."**

King David is best known for:
- slaying Goliath
- being Israel's greatest earthy king
- passionate psalmist and musician
- repentant heart

Focus: Central Verse / Passage

In the beginning of 1 Samuel, we learn that Hannah was childless, praying fervently before the Lord for a son. God answers and gives her Samuel. **Read her prayer of thanksgiving in 1 Samuel 2:1-10.**

Write down some of the ways she describes God:

_____
_____
_____
_____

What prophetic anticipation can we see toward the end of her prayer and declaration before God?

_____
_____

" *HE WILL GIVE STRENGTH TO HIS KING AND EXALT THE HORN OF HIS ANOINTED.* — **1 SAMUEL 2:10** "

Memory verse for lesson:
But the Lord said to Samuel, "Do not look at his appearance or at his physical stature, because I have refused him. For the Lord does not see as man sees; for man looks at the outward appearance, but the Lord looks at the heart" (1 Samuel 16:7 NKJV).

THE ?ARADOXICAL JESUS in 1 SAMUEL

We know the Bible does not contradict itself, so it is important we take time to study and understand all sides of the truth and interpret Scripture in light of Scripture to understand.

Reread the following verse:
"Now the Spirit of the LORD had departed from Saul, and an evil spirit from the LORD tormented him" (1 Samuel 16:14).

What are some of the tensions about this verse that could lead someone to believe the Bible contradicts itself?

_____
_____
_____

Do you believe this compromises God's love for Saul? How do we reconcile a Loving God using an evil spirit to torment an anointed king?

_____
_____
_____
_____

How does this verse resolve to ultimately show God's supremacy?

_____
_____
_____

I saw Jesus more clearly in this book when...

JESUS UP CLOSE:

LESSON 10

2 SAMUEL: THE DELIVERER

In your SEEING JESUS Study Guide:
Read through the fast facts, author and setting, and overview on page 101 and 102. Reflect and take notes.

Jesus in 2 Samuel:

1 and 2 Samuel were originally one book. David's 40-year reign is covered in this book, showing the king's strengths and weaknesses. He is the only one called, "a man after God's own heart." David knew Jesus in an intimate way. Jesus quoted the psalms written by David throughout his earthly ministry.

Read the passage below. Underline the verses where you can "see" Jesus through David's praiseful words.

2 Samuel 22:1-20

David sang to the LORD the words of this song when the LORD delivered him from the hand of all his enemies and from the hand of Saul.

2 He said: "The LORD is my rock, my fortress and my deliverer; **3** my God is my rock, in whom I take refuge, my shield and the horn of my salvation. He is my stronghold, my refuge and my savior-- from violent men you save me. **4** I call to the LORD, who is worthy of praise, and I am saved from my enemies.

5 "The waves of death swirled about me; the torrents of destruction overwhelmed me. **6** The cords of the grave coiled around me; the snares of death confronted me. **7** In my distress I called to the LORD; I called out to my God. From his temple he heard my voice; my cry came to his ears.

> *THE LORD IS MY ROCK, MY FORTRESS AND MY DELIVERER; MY GOD IS MY ROCK, IN WHOM I TAKE REFUGE, MY SHIELD AND THE HORN OF MY SALVATION. HE IS MY STRONGHOLD, MY REFUGE AND MY SAVIOR.*

8 "The earth trembled and quaked, the foundations of the heavens shook; they trembled because he was angry. **9** Smoke rose from his nostrils; consuming fire came from his mouth, burning coals blazed out of it. **10** He parted the heavens and came down; dark clouds were under his feet. **11** He mounted the cherubim and flew; he soared on the wings of the wind. **12** He made darkness his canopy around him—the dark rain clouds of the sky. **13** Out of the brightness of his presence bolts of lightning blazed forth. **14** The LORD thundered from heaven; the voice of the Most High resounded. **15** He shot arrows and scattered [the enemies], bolts of lightning and routed them. **16** The valleys of the sea were exposed and the foundations of the earth laid bare at the rebuke of the LORD, at the blast of breath from his nostrils.

17 "He reached down from on high and took hold of me; he drew me out of deep waters. **18** He rescued me from my powerful enemy, from my foes, who were too strong for me. **19** They confronted me in the day of my disaster, but the LORD was my support. **20** He brought me out into a spacious place; he rescued me because he delighted in me.

Reflection Exercises:
What was David's first response after being delivered from Saul?

In 1 Samuel 13:14 we hear the Lord's rebuke to Saul and David is called "a man after God's own heart." In studying the life of David, as shepherd, psalmist, king, warrior, why do you think this description was given to him?

How does David describe the ways the Lord has delivered him (see also Psalm 18)?

What are some of the reasons David gives for praising the Lord?

Write your own psalm that describes how Jesus has delivered you and saved you from your enemies.

Unpacking the Outline:
See the lesson outline for 2 Samuel on page 102 and 103 of your study guide.

Read God's promise to David and David's prayer in 2 Samuel 7.

List some of the things God promised David through Nathan the prophet:

1.
2.
3.
4.
5.

How do we see God's sovereign choice to redeem Israel in this passage?

> **WHO AM I, SOVEREIGN LORD, AND WHAT IS MY FAMILY, THAT YOU HAVE BROUGHT ME THIS FAR?** — **2 SAMUEL 7:18B**

Focus: Central Verse / Passage

At the end of David's reign, he writes what is known as the "last words of David." King David knew that when a king reigned in righteousness, the people were safe. This prophetic word would only be fully realized in the reign of Jesus. God promised David's descendants would be blessed.

> **IS NOT MY HOUSE RIGHT WITH GOD? HAS HE NOT MADE WITH ME AN EVERLASTING COVENANT, ARRANGED AND SECURED IN EVERY PART? WILL HE NOT BRING TO FRUITION MY SALVATION AND GRANT ME MY EVERY DESIRE?** — **2 SAMUEL 23:5**

Throughout his rule, we know David was not a perfect father or husband. He sinned miserably in these areas. But the Lord extended forgiveness because of His grace. How has God extended grace unexpectedly in your family?

How do we see the grace of Jesus in David in more marked ways than anyone else so far in our journey through the Bible?

Memory verse for lesson:
And now, O Lord God, You are God, and Your words are true, and You have promised this goodness to Your servant. Now therefore, let it please You to bless the house of Your servant, that it may continue forever before You; for You, O Lord God, have spoken it, and with Your blessing let the house of Your servant be blessed forever (2 Samuel 7:28-29 NKJV).

THE ?ARADOXICAL JESUS in 2 SAMUEL

We know the Bible does not contradict itself, so it is important to take time to study and understand all sides of the truth and interpret Scripture in light of Scripture to grasp the whole truth as much as possible.

Read 1 Samuel 13:14:
"the Lord has sought out a man after his own heart and appointed him leader of his people, because you have not kept the Lord's command."

Read 1 Samuel 11:2-4:
"One evening David got up from his bed and walked around on the roof of the palace. From the roof he saw a woman bathing. The woman was very beautiful, and David sent someone to find out about her. ...She came to him, and he slept with her."

We know David sinned greatly in the eyes of the Lord and God sends Nathan, the prophet, to rebuke David. What tensions rise up when we grapple with David's adultery and murdering Bathsheba's husband, Uriah?

Should this dismiss God's honorable words we read in 1 Samuel 13:14?

44

Refer above to some of the answers you wrote out explaining why you believe God called David "a man after his own heart." Do any of your reasons listed help with this tension?

_____
_____
_____
_____
_____

How does David's story offer hope to all of us?

_____
_____
_____
_____
_____

I saw Jesus more clearly in this book when...

_____
_____
_____
_____

JESUS UP CLOSE:

KINGS AND PROPHETS 1
VIDEO SEGMENT LESSON GUIDE

INTRODUCTION TO *SEEING JESUS* (10-15 MINUTES):
We will be looking at the ministry of Elijah and Elisha in this study. Elijah is one of the Bible's most renowned prophets. He is mentioned in the New Testament in various places and appears to Jesus on the Mount of Transfiguration. James 5:17-18 shows his strong prayer life. When God gave him a word, He followed through with prayer, not just waiting passively. James 5 says Elijah was human as we are.

What miracles are you praying for right now? Or, what miracles would you like to ask God for that you've hesitated to pray about?

_____
_____
_____
_____

ELIJAH AND ELISHA:
God sends his best prophets to the worst kings! Because of God's love, He sends His best to the worst.

1. Elijah predicts a _____ .
2. He warned _____ but he flees.
3. _____ brought him food and the brook dries up.
4. He sends Elijah to a _____ .

1 Kings 17-19:

Zarephath: widow, also home of Jezebel.

Miracle of the meal and oil.

The widow's son dies, but Elijah raises her son from the dead.

Ahab and Jezebel worshipping Baal and Elijah challenges their gods.

God is dealing with the Northern Kingdom.

Elijah builds an altar. He takes twelve stones because God wants twelve tribes.

The Baal prophets then build an altar, wailing and cutting themselves.

God answers by fire! This leads the Israelites to recommit their lives to God.

Elijah prays for rain. The servant checks the sky six times.

He comes back the seventh time and says, "A cloud as small as a man's hand is rising from the sea." I Kings 18:44

(Elijah's prayers touching heaven).

And then scripture says, "The hand of the Lord came upon him."

Two Hands signify:

It rained, and it rained, and it rained!

After Mt. Carmel:

Elijah runs into the wilderness because Jezebel wants to kill him.

    angel comes

    he sleeps

    he's exhausted

God didn't want Elijah to stay in his depression.

God has faithful people everywhere, even when we feel alone.

God told him He had 7,000 prophets who have never bowed down to Baal. (I Kings 19:18)

The Lord gives Elijah another assignment in the cave. Someone is going to come after you.

Elisha –

The prophets are waiting for Elijah's rapture. He asks for a double portion of Elijah's spirit.

Chariots of the Lord came and separated Elijah and Elisha. Elijah drops his mantle and Elisha grabs it.

Elisha's first miracle: Jordan River opens for Elisha

"I counted the number of miracles of Elijah and Elisha and the miracles of Elisha are exactly double" – Marilyn

    Moabite –

What is the mantle Jesus dropped down for you and me? The Holy Spirit. The Holy Spirit is for the miraculous.

Reminder: The anointing of God is for us to move in its power.

Application lesson: Don't bury your mantle.

Jesus Sightings in the Lives of His prophets (15 minutes):

Review Elijah's and Elisha's miracles on pages 121-122 of study guide. Marilyn mentioned Elisha's miracles were exactly double. Compare and contrast the ministry of the two prophets. Scripture says we are to imitate the faith of the faithful.

How can we see Elijah's ministry through Elisha's?

What was Elijah's weakness according to what we've studied so far?

Why do you think Elijah feared Jezebel as he did, after seeing God's power at Mt. Carmel, defeating 450 prophets of Baal?

Marilyn challenges participants to write down four miracles that you are believing God to accomplish. Sometimes we do not see miracles simply because we don't ask. Prayerfully consider four that the Lord is impressing on your heart.

Miracles:

1. _____
2. _____
3. _____
4. _____

*Make a note to revisit these at the end of the study and share what answers God has given you through exercising your faith!

LESSON 11

1 KINGS: GOD'S RECORDS

In your SEEING JESUS Study Guide:
Read through the fast facts, author and setting, and overview on page 106 and 107. Reflect and take notes.

Jesus in 1 Kings:

Solomon's reign gives us a glimpse of Jesus Christ in many ways. Solomon's resources, wisdom, and honor foreshadow, in part, Christ's kingdom. This book shows the dynamics between a king's leadership and the people. This book is more than a political report of history. First Kings records Israel's spiritual response to their God, a covenant people blessed through David's lineage.

From reading 2 Samuel, we know that David desired to build a temple for the Lord, but the Lord said no. The Lord allowed David's son, Solomon, to build the temple where the ark of the covenant would reside. Solomon began his reign at age 20, half the age of when David became king. The Lord appeared to Solomon in the night asking him to ask whatever he wished.

Read Solomon's prayer to the Lord. Circle or underline words and phrases that foreshadow Jesus' kingdom being established through Solomon.

1 Kings 3:5-15 – Solomon's Dream

At Gibeon the LORD appeared to Solomon during the night in a dream, and God said, "Ask for whatever you want me to give you." **6** Solomon answered, "You have shown great kindness to your servant, my father David, because he was faithful to you and righteous and upright in heart. You have continued this great kindness to him

> *I WILL DO WHAT YOU HAVE ASKED. I WILL GIVE YOU A WISE AND DISCERNING HEART, SO THAT THERE WILL NEVER HAVE BEEN ANYONE LIKE YOU, NOR WILL THERE EVER BE....*

and have given him a son to sit on his throne this very day. **7** "Now, O LORD my God, you have made your servant king in place of my father David. But I am only a little child and do not know how to carry out my duties. **8** Your servant is here among the people you have chosen, a great people, too numerous to count or number. **9** So give your servant a discerning heart to govern your people and to distinguish between right and wrong. For who is able to govern this great people of yours?" **10** The Lord was pleased that Solomon had asked for this. **11** So God said to him, "Since you have asked for this and not for long life or wealth for yourself, nor have asked for the death of your enemies but for discernment in administering justice, **12** I will do what you have asked. I will give you a wise and discerning heart, so that there will never have been anyone like you, nor will there ever be. **13** Moreover, I will give you what you have not asked for--both riches and honor--so that in your lifetime you will have no equal among kings. **14** And if you walk in my ways and obey my statutes and commands as David your father did, I will give you a long life." **15** Then Solomon awoke and he realized it had been a dream. He returned to Jerusalem, stood before the ark of the Lord's covenant and sacrificed burnt offerings and fellowship offerings. Then he gave a feast for all his court.

Reflection Exercises:
What did God tell Solomon he could ask for?

_____
_____
_____
_____

Paraphrase and write out Solomon's request to the Lord:

_____
_____
_____
_____
_____
_____
_____

What were the things God promised to do in light of Solomon's request?

_____
_____
_____
_____
_____
_____

Write out some phrases that show similarities between Solomon and David in this passage.

_____
_____
_____
_____
_____
_____

Unpacking the Outline:
See the chart overview for 1 Kings on page 106 of your study guide.

In the first eleven chapters, the life and reign of Solomon is recorded, ending on the consequences of his sinfulness.

Read over 1 Kings 11.

List some of the things that caused Solomon's kingdom to weaken:

1. _____
2. _____
3. _____
4. _____
5. _____

Focus: Central Verse / Passage
1 Kings 10:23-24

King Solomon was greater in riches and wisdom than all the other kings of the earth. The whole world sought audience with Solomon to hear the wisdom God had put in his heart.

How do we see the grace of Jesus more markedly in David's life than anyone else so far in our journey?

_____
_____
_____
_____
_____

Memory Verse for lesson:

Now if you walk before Me as your father David walked, in integrity of heart and in uprightness, to do according to all that I have commanded you, and if you keep My statutes and My judgments, then I will establish the throne of your kingdom over Israel forever, as I promised (1 Kings 9:4-5a NKJV).

THE ?ARADOXICAL JESUS in 1 KINGS

We know the Bible does not contradict itself, so it is important to take time to study and understand all sides of the truth and interpret Scripture in light of Scripture to grasp the whole truth as much as possible.

Read the following verses:

"King Solomon was greater in riches and wisdom than all the other kings of the earth" (1 Kings 10:23).

"King Solomon, however, loved many foreign women besides Pharoah's daughter…They were from nations the Lord had told the Israelites, 'You must not intermarry with them, because they will surely turn your hearts after their gods.' Nevertheless, Solomon held fast to them in love. He had seven hundred wives …." (1 Kings 11:1-3a).

King Solomon was declared the wisest king, yet his actions proved to be unwise. When you see how he went against God's wishes and married women who worshipped foreign gods, it seems Solomon could be called the most foolish king of all.

Does his sin take away from the gift of wisdom he had?

_____
_____
_____
_____
_____

53

What is the difference between wisdom and knowledge?

___

Solomon wrote most of Proverbs. Read over Proverbs 5, keeping in mind Solomon had 700 wives and 300 concubines. How might his sagely sayings have helped him in straying from what God intended, to have one wife.

I saw Jesus more clearly in this book when...
___

JESUS UP CLOSE:

54

KINGS AND PROPHETS 2
VIDEO SEGMENT LESSON GUIDE

INTRODUCTION TO *SEEING JESUS* (10-15 MINUTES):
Our study is just beginning on the reign of kings over the Divided Kingdom. Think about the kings we've studied through Solomon. What were their failures and strengths? After the Kingdom is divided, we see much more wickedness rising in the hearts of kings.

How do fractions among God's people cause weakness?

_____
_____
_____
_____

Watch video segment (Approx. 20-30 minutes). Take notes and fill in the blanks.

Solomon -

1. Solomon was the son of _____ .

God's puts his hand on Solomon to be king.

> *DID YOU EVER TRY TO HELP GOD?* — **MARILYN**

Adonijah -

2. David and Bathsheba put _____ into Solomon. Whatever you do, get _____ .

Note: Proverbs is written to be sung.

3. Solomon asked for _____ and _____ .

God was pleased and promised wisdom, understanding, and long life.

Solomon is very involved in the wisdom books of the Bible: Psalms, Proverbs, Song of Solomon, Ecclesiastes. Solomon went after godly wisdom....but he turned.

What caused Solomon's detour?

_____
_____
_____
_____

Solomon's wives:

Remember: Faith always pleases God.

>> *Fact:* The House of David has never ended! ...even with all the bad kings.

What God builds He keeps: what we build can fall apart.

4. Solomon's temple lasted maybe _____ years.

Even wisdom can't keep us from falling away from God.

Solomon compromised his life with idolatry.

Key: God is the source of our blessings.

5. Solomon does repent at the end of his life. He held on to the _____ .

STOP: Turn to page 127 in study guide and see chart on The Divided Kingdom: (Marilyn instructs on good and bad kings)

God makes prophets to go with kings.

Prophets: Samuel, Nathan, Gad. They help kings rule in a righteous way.

Rehoboam takes Solomon's place and lacks wisdom.

Rules without relationship cause rebellion.
Ten tribes leave Rehoboam. Only Judah and Benjamin remain with him.
Rehoboam had mixed parenting.

Prophets come to guide and Rehoboam rejects God's wisdom.

Application: As we follow the kings and prophets, write down the lessons you are learning.

Jesus Sightings in Kings and Chronicles (15 minutes):
David had one of the greatest revelations about Jesus. He wrote the 23rd Psalm before he battled Goliath. We also know his shortcomings and his sin with Bathsheba. In response to his sin, he wrote Psalm 51.

Take time here to read Psalm 23. If you are too familiar with it, try reading in another version. What does this psalm reveal about David's understanding of who God is?

_____
_____
_____
_____

What are some of the ways we see that David had God's anointing?

Read aloud as a group Psalm 51. List David's requests before in response to his sin?

How does this psalm reveal the grace of Jesus Christ?

Wrap Up (10-15 minutes):
In looking at Saul and David, we can see success and failure in their kingship. John 15:5 says that apart from Jesus Christ, we can do nothing. He gives us the anointing to do things beyond our ability. As Marilyn suggested, write out some of the ways you discern God has anointed you for service. (If your group is well acquainted with one another, maybe have your group share what they see in each other) Ask the Lord to use the list below in greater ways. Share some barriers that have caused you to not walk in His anointing.

Spend time sharing prayer requests and closing in prayer.

LESSON 12

2 KINGS: GOD'S RECORDS

In your SEEING JESUS Study Guide:
Read through the fast facts, author and setting, and overview on page 108 and 109. Reflect and take notes.

Jesus in 2 Kings:

Second Kings records the kings of Israel and Judah. We also see the prophetic transition of Elijah and Elisha. The Lord sent prophets to help guide and speak to the kings.

Elijah's last journey begins with him walking with Elisha, his successor. In the first eight chapters of 2 Kings, we read about Elisha's ministry and miracles. He asked for a double portion of his spirit. Circle and underline the miracles of Elijah and Elisha that show their likeness to Jesus.

Read 2 Kings 2:7-18

Fifty men from the company of the prophets went and stood at a distance, facing the place where Elijah and Elisha had stopped at the Jordan. **8** Elijah took his cloak, rolled it up and struck the water with it. The water divided to the right and to the left, and the two of them crossed over on dry ground.

9 When they had crossed, Elijah said to Elisha, "Tell me, what can I do for you before I am taken from you?" "Let me inherit a double portion of your spirit," Elisha replied.

10 "You have asked a difficult thing," Elijah said, "yet if you see me when I am taken from you, it will be yours—otherwise, it will not."

11 As they were walking along and talking together, suddenly a chariot of fire and horses of fire appeared and separated the two of them, and Elijah went up to heaven in a whirlwind. **12** Elisha saw this and cried out, "My father! My father! The chariots and horsemen of Israel!" And Elisha saw him no more. Then he took hold of his garment and tore it in two. **13** Elisha then picked up Elijah's cloak that had fallen from him and went back and stood on the bank of the Jordan. **14** He took the cloak that had fallen from Elijah and struck the water with it. "Where now is the Lord, the God of Elijah?" he asked. When he struck the water, it divided to the right and to the left, and he crossed over. **15** The company of the prophets from Jericho, who were watching, said, "The spirit of Elijah is resting on Elisha." And they went to meet him and bowed to the ground before him. **16** "Look," they said, "we your servants have fifty able men. Let them go and look for your master. Perhaps the Spirit of the Lord has picked him up and set him down on some mountain or in some valley." "No," Elisha replied, "do not send them."

17 But they persisted until he was too embarrassed to refuse. So he said, "Send them." And they sent fifty men, who searched for three days but did not find him. 18 When they returned to Elisha, who was staying in Jericho, he said to them, "Didn't I tell you not to go?"

Reflection Exercises:

Why do you think Elisha asked for a double-portion from his teacher?

_____
_____
_____
_____

What is the "suddenly" moment recorded in this passage?

_____
_____
_____
_____

The fifty other prophets recognized Elijah's mantle had transferred to Elisha, but they struggled to believe that Elijah escaped death, as this was very difficult to comprehend. How does their response parallel the disciples when the tomb was found empty?

_____
_____
_____
_____

Scripture records Elisha to have administered twice as many miracles as Elijah. Read over a few listed below. How were some of these miracles similar to the ones Jesus performed?

1. Cleaning the waters of the river (2 Kings 2:19-22): _____
   _____

2. Widow's supply (2 Kings 4:1-7): _____
   _____

3. Barren woman, resurrects dead son (2 Kings 4:8-37): _____
   _____

4. Multiplies loaves (2 Kings 4:4:42-44): _____
   _____

Unpacking the Outline:
Review the chart on page 108 of the study guide. Godly kings emerge in Judah, but the bad outweighed righteous kings.

Josiah was the last good king before the kingdom was destroyed. List some of the good things he did. See 2 Kings 22-24:

1. _____
2. _____
3. _____
4. _____
5. _____

THREE PROMINENT THEMES IN 2 KINGS:
1. The Lord will judge His people
2. The word of His prophets always comes to pass
3. God is faithful, even when His people are unfaithful.

Focus: Central Verse / Passage
2 Kings 17:7-8

All this took place because the Israelites had sinned against the Lord their God, who had brought them up out of Egypt from under the power of Pharaoh king of Egypt. They worshiped other gods and followed the practices of the nations the Lord had driven out before them, as well as the practices that the kings of Israel had introduced.

Nineteen consecutive evil kings ruled in Israel through its history. All worshipped other gods, allowing the nation to become vulnerable to idolatry. List five of the evil kings and their sin against God. See 2 Kings 8-17.

1. _____
2. _____
3. _____
4. _____
5. _____

Memory Verse for lesson:

And he did what was right in the sight of the Lord, and walked in all the ways of his father David; he did not turn aside to the right hand or to the left (2 Kings 22:2 NKJV).

THE ?ARADOXICAL JESUS in 2 KINGS

We know the Bible does not contradict itself, so it is important to take time to study and understand all sides of the truth and interpret Scripture in light of Scripture to grasp the whole truth as much as possible.

Hezekiah and Josiah were good kings who fostered revival in Judah, and the other kings sought security with the nations around them. The Lord remained faithful to His promise to David through Jehoiachin.

Read Proverbs 21:1:
"The king's heart is in the hand of the Lord, Like the rivers of water; He turns it wherever He wishes"

How do we reconcile this proverb with the history of 1 and 2 Kings?

_____
_____
_____
_____

I saw Jesus more clearly in this book when…

_____
_____
_____

JESUS UP CLOSE:

LESSON 13

1 CHRONICLES: REVIEWING DAVID'S KINGDOM

In your SEEING JESUS Study Guide:
Read through the fast facts, author and setting, and overview on page 110 and 111. Reflect and take notes.

Jesus in 1 Chronicles:

The book of 1 Chronicles reveals the truth of God's faithfulness. Ezra, the scribe, wrote this book, showing humanity's failures, but God's perfect love. The emphasis is on David's dynasty as he takes the throne. Ezra was a strong historian and over 50% of the text of Chronicles shows parallels with other portions of the Old Testament.

We read about David's private anointing in Lesson 11 with Samuel, and now we read of the death of King Saul and David's public reign over Israel. God surrounded David with the right support through David's Mighty Men.

Read over the following passage. Circle and underline how this foreshadows the functioning of the Body of Christ:

David Becomes King Over Israel – 1 Chronicles 11:1-25

All Israel came together to David at Hebron and said, "We are your own flesh and blood. **2** In the past, even while Saul was king, you were the one who led Israel on their military campaigns. And the Lord your God said to you, 'You will shepherd my people Israel, and you will become their ruler.'"

3 When all the elders of Israel had come to King David at Hebron, he made a covenant with them at Hebron before the Lord, and they anointed David king over Israel, as the Lord had promised through Samuel.

David Conquers Jerusalem

4 David and all the Israelites marched to Jerusalem (that is, Jebus). The Jebusites who lived there **5** said to David, "You will not get in here." Nevertheless, David captured the fortress of Zion—which is the City of David.

6 David had said, "Whoever leads the attack on the Jebusites will become commander-in-chief." Joab son of Zeruiah went up first, and so he received the command.

7 David then took up residence in the fortress, and so it was called the City of David. **8** He built up the city around it, from the terraces to the surrounding wall, while Joab restored the rest of the city. **9** And David became more and more powerful, because the Lord Almighty was with him.

David's Mighty Warriors

10 These were the chiefs of David's mighty warriors—they, together with all Israel, gave his kingship strong support to extend it over the whole land, as the Lord had promised— **11** this is the list of David's mighty warriors:

Jashobeam, a Hakmonite, was chief of the officers; he raised his spear against three hundred men, whom he killed in one encounter.

12 Next to him was Eleazar son of Dodai the Ahohite, one of the three mighty warriors. **13** He was with David at Pas Dammim when the Philistines gathered there for battle. At a place where there was a field full of barley, the troops fled from the Philistines. **14** But they took their stand in the middle of the field. They defended it and struck the Philistines down, and the Lord brought about a great victory.

15 Three of the thirty chiefs came down to David to the rock at the cave of Adullam, while a band of Philistines was encamped in the Valley of Rephaim. **16** At that time David was in the stronghold, and the Philistine garrison was at Bethlehem. **17** David longed for water and said, "Oh, that someone would get me a drink of water from the well near the gate of Bethlehem!" **18** So the Three broke through the Philistine lines, drew water from the well near the gate of Bethlehem and carried it back to David. But he refused to drink it; instead, he poured it out to the Lord. **19** "God forbid that I should do this!" he said. "Should I drink the blood of these men who went at the risk of their lives?" Because they risked their lives to bring it back, David would not drink it.

Such were the exploits of the three mighty warriors.

20 Abishai the brother of Joab was chief of the Three. He raised his spear against three hundred men, whom he killed, and so he became as famous as the Three. **21** He was doubly honored above the Three and became their commander, even though he was not included among them.

22 Benaiah son of Jehoiada, a valiant fighter from Kabzeel, performed great exploits. He struck down two mightiest warriors. He also went down into a pit on a snowy day and killed a lion. **23** And he struck down an Egyptian who was five cubits tall. Although the Egyptian had a spear like a weaver's rod in his hand, Benaiah went against him with a club. He snatched the spear from the Egyptian's hand and killed him with his own spear. **24** Such were the exploits of Benaiah son of Jehoiada; he too was as famous as the three mighty warriors. **25** He was held in greater honor than any of the Thirty, but he was not included among the Three. And David put him in charge of his bodyguard.

Reflection Exercises:

Read verses 10-11. What was the role of David's Mighty Men, according to these verses?

_____
_____
_____
_____

List some of the exploits of David's men. What victories strengthened David's throne?

_____
_____
_____
_____
_____

Read verses 20-25, about the exploits of Abishai and Benaiah. Though they were not included in the three chiefs, their defeats were legendary. Summarize their victories and the unique ways they conquered the enemies of Israel.

_____
_____
_____
_____
_____

> **AND DAVID BECAME MORE AND MORE POWERFUL, BECAUSE THE LORD ALMIGHTY WAS WITH HIM. — 1 CHRONICLES 11:9**

Read Psalm 133, written by David. David knew that brotherly unity would fortify Israel. The enemy knows it is easier to attack when there is division among His people. How can we as believers learn to live in unity better in the life of the church?

_____
_____

Unpacking the Outline:
See page 110 in your study guide to review the chart overview of the book.

God chose prophets to walk alongside kings, to counsel, exhort, and rebuke. God promised King David that He would settle him and His throne through the prophet. Read 1 Chronicles 17:11-14. List the promises of God given to David.

1. _____
2. _____
3. _____
4. _____
5. _____

Ezra honors the transcendent majesty of God (1 Chronicles 29:11) and quotes statements from past history describing him as Ruler over all.

Focus: Central Verse / Passage
1 Chronicles 29:10-14

King David didn't hesitate to publicly praise God. He encouraged corporate worship through his prayer life:

10 David praised the Lord in the presence of the whole assembly, saying, "Praise be to you, O Lord, God of our father Israel, from everlasting to everlasting. **11** Yours, O Lord, is the greatness and the power and the glory and the majesty and the splendor, for everything in heaven and earth is yours. Yours, O Lord, is the kingdom; you are exalted as head over all. **12** Wealth and honor come from you; you are the ruler of all things. In your hands are strength and power to exalt and give strength to all. **13** Now, our God, we give you thanks, and praise your glorious name. **14** "But who am I, and who are my people, that we should be able to give as generously as this? Everything comes from you, and we have given you only what comes from your hand."

A prayer journal reveals a lot about a person. What we pray for reveals our thoughts about God and others. What does this passage reveal about David's heart? How did He view God? Himself?

_____
_____
_____
_____
_____

Memory Verse for Lesson:
Both riches and honor come from You, And You reign over all. In Your hand is power and might; In Your hand it is to make great and to give strength to all (1 Chronicles 29:12 NKJV).

THE ?ARADOXICAL JESUS in 1 CHRONICLES

We know the Bible does not contradict itself, so it is important to take time to study and understand all sides of the truth and interpret Scripture in light of Scripture to grasp the whole truth as much as possible.

1 Chronicles closes with the death of David. Sometimes we see God's chosen leaders meet death finishing well and others not finishing well. David's flaws have been revealed and not hidden in God's Word. And it seems God judges people based upon the king in place. The burden of obedience seems to rely heavily on the shoulders of a king. And a king is usually warned by a prophet.

How does this model cause tension in your understanding of grace?

___

Is it fair for God to punish a people based on a Ruler's reign? Why or why not?

___

I saw Jesus more clearly in this book when...

___

JESUS UP CLOSE:

KINGS AND PROPHETS 3
VIDEO SEGMENT LESSON GUIDE

INTRODUCTION TO *SEEING JESUS* (10-15 MINUTES):
Our study is just beginning on the reign of kings over the Divided Kingdom. Think about the kings we've studied through Solomon. What were their failures and strengths? After the Kingdom is divided, we see much more wickedness rising in the hearts of kings. How do fractions among God's people cause more vulnerabilities?

Watch video segment (Approx. 20-30 minutes). Take notes and fill in the blanks:

Opening Prayer: "Father, in Jesus' Name, give me seeing eyes."

Dynasties:

ISRAEL - NORTHERN KINGDOM   JUDAH - SOUTHERN KINGDOM

Turn to page 127 in your *Seeing Jesus* study guide:

Rehoboam (bad king) –

1. Key point: Prophets are involved to make us _____ , to help us see Jesus more than ever before.

Golden calves of Jeroboam:

Nadab –

2. Reminder: Judah's line is from the genealogy of _____ .

Southern King, Asa (good king) –

Northern King Baasha (bad king) –

3. King Baasha was an _____ .

Did any prophets come to warn them?

_____
_____
_____
_____

Jehoshaphat makes a compromise with the Northern Kingdom. He wants peace with the Northern Kingdom and comes into an alliance with Ahab.

Life lesson from Jehoshapat: He should have never compromised the Kingdom for false peace.

Take notes on the following kings and draw lines of connections that Marilyn makes.

    Ahab (Jezebel is his wife) –

    Athaliah (daughter of Jezebel) – takes throne of Northern kingdom

Be careful about compromise. Mixed marriages cause strife: It is not good to marry unbelievers.

A godly priest comes along in godly providence.

    King Jehoash (good king) – nurtured by a godly priest.

STOP! Review of 1 and 2 Kings & 1 and 2 Chronicles:
Chronicles stresses David's dynasty

Jesus Sightings in the Divided Kingdom (15 minutes):
Review some of your notes on page 127-128. In this video segment, we can see more clearly the impact the kings from the North and the South had on each other. We even see God's grace in the lineage of Ahab and Jezebel. God always redeems, even the worst of hearts and circumstances because of His grace.

    With some of the points made in the video segment, how did God bring about grace to even bad kings in unexpected ways?

_____
_____
_____
_____

    Take a moment to review Asa and Rehoboam. What godly marks were left of their reign? How did they follow God?

_____
_____
_____
_____

Marilyn mentions King Baasha and King Elah struggled with alcoholism. Think about your own family tree. Where can you see generational sin take hold? When have you experienced God's grace take over and break it?

___

Wrap Up (10-15 minutes):
We can learn a lot from the public failure of kings and rulers, but also we can learn from their successes. As Marilyn challenged viewers in closing, write down safeguards for your life that will keep you moving in the right direction with God. Identify four things you know that will lead you in the wrong direction. Share your insights.

Right direction:

1.

2.

3.

4.

Wrong direction:

1.

2.

3.

4.

LESSON 14

2 CHRONICLES: REVIEWING DAVID'S KINGDOM

In your SEEING JESUS Study Guide:
Read through the fast facts, author and setting, and overview on page 113 - 115. Reflect and take notes.

Jesus in 2 Chronicles:

Just as 1 Chronicles parallels 1 and 2 Samuel, 2 Chronicles parallels 1 and 2 Kings. The beginning of the book begins with Solomon's inauguration and success. Solomon's silver and gold were as common as stones (2 Chronicles 1:15). We see that Solomon was firmly established and God made him "exceedingly great" (see 1 Chronicles 29:25). Read the following passage and circle or underline how we can see Jesus in the building of the new temple. The Temple is a type of Christ Himself (Matthew 12:6; John 2:19; Revelation 21:22).

Solomon's Temple - 2 Chronicles 2:1-18

Solomon gave orders to build a temple for the Name of the Lord and a royal palace for himself. **2** He conscripted 70,000 men as carriers and 80,000 as stonecutters in the hills and 3,600 as foremen over them.

3 Solomon sent this message to Hiram king of Tyre:
"Send me cedar logs as you did for my father David when you sent him cedar to build a palace to live in. **4** Now I am about to build a temple for the Name of the Lord my God and to dedicate it to him for burning fragrant incense before him, for setting out the consecrated bread regularly, and for making burnt offerings every morning and evening and on the Sabbaths, at the New Moons and at the appointed festivals of the Lord our God. This is a lasting ordinance for Israel.

5 "The temple I am going to build will be great, because our God is greater than all other gods. **6** But who is able to

> *PRAISE BE TO THE LORD, THE GOD OF ISRAEL, WHO MADE HEAVEN AND EARTH! HE HAS GIVEN KING DAVID A WISE SON, ENDOWED WITH INTELLIGENCE AND DISCERNMENT, WHO WILL BUILD A TEMPLE FOR THE LORD AND A PALACE FOR HIMSELF.*

build a temple for him, since the heavens, even the highest heavens, cannot contain him? Who then am I to build a temple for him, except as a place to burn sacrifices before him?

7 "Send me, therefore, a man skilled to work in gold and silver, bronze and iron, and in purple, crimson and blue yarn, and experienced in the art of engraving, to work in Judah and Jerusalem with my skilled workers, whom my father David provided.

8 "Send me also cedar, juniper and algum logs from Lebanon, for I know that your servants are skilled in cutting timber there. My servants will work with yours **9** to provide me with plenty of lumber, because the temple I build must be large and magnificent. **10** I will give your servants, the woodsmen who cut the timber, twenty thousand cors of ground wheat, twenty thousand cors of barley, twenty thousand baths of wine and twenty thousand baths of olive oil."

11 Hiram king of Tyre replied by letter to Solomon:
"Because the Lord loves his people, he has made you their king."

12 And Hiram added:
"Praise be to the Lord, the God of Israel, who made heaven and earth! He has given King David a wise son, endowed with intelligence and discernment, who will build a temple for the Lord and a palace for himself.

13 "I am sending you Huram-Abi, a man of great skill, **14** whose mother was from Dan and whose father was from Tyre. He is trained to work in gold and silver, bronze and iron, stone and wood, and with purple and blue and crimson yarn and fine linen. He is experienced in all kinds of engraving and can execute any design given to him. He will work with your skilled workers and with those of my lord, David your father.

15 "Now let my lord send his servants the wheat and barley and the olive oil and wine he promised, **16** and we will cut all the logs from Lebanon that you need and will float them as rafts by sea down to Joppa. You can then take them up to Jerusalem."

17 Solomon took a census of all the foreigners residing in Israel, after the census his father David had taken; and they were found to be 153,600. **18** He assigned 70,000 of them to be carriers and 80,000 to be stonecutters in the hills, with 3,600 foremen over them to keep the people working.

Reflection Exercises:

Review some of the words you circled or underlined. Jesus came as the chief cornerstone which our worship is centered upon. Though Solomon is noted for his great wealth, the building of the Temple was viewed in his day as the most important legacy. What concerns did Solomon say to show how seriously he took this assignment?

_____
_____
_____
_____

Think about the barriers you face in maintaining an attitude of worship. What things distract us from worshiping God in spirit and truth today?

_____
_____
_____
_____

For the Israelites the purpose of the Temple was to host the presence of God. In our church life today, it is easy to see the church as just an event. They directly tied it to their salvation. Do you think we have lost some of the importance of corporate worship?

_____
_____
_____
_____

2 Chronicles (also 1 and 2 Kings) ignores the Northern Kingdom due to their unfaithfulness for worshiping other gods and ignoring the Temple. Seventy percent of the book deals with the good kings.

> *AND THE PRIESTS COULD NOT PERFORM THEIR SERVICE BECAUSE OF THE CLOUD, FOR THE GLORY OF THE LORD FILLED THE TEMPLE OF GOD.*
> *– 2 CHRONICLES 5:14*

Unpacking the Outline:
Review page 117 in the study guide. Pick one of the following and study their rule and reign. Determine if they were a good or bad king according to scripture:

REHOBOAM • JEHOSHAPHAT • ASA • JOSIAH

1. _____
2. _____
3. _____
4. _____
5. _____

How can we see generational sin appear in the lineage of the kings?

🔍 Focus: Central Verse / Passage
2 Chronicles 20:15

"He said: 'Listen, King Jehoshaphat and all who live in Judah and Jerusalem! This is what the Lord says to you: Do not be afraid or discouraged because of this vast army. For the battle is not yours, but God's.'"

What was the situation surrounding this battle?

What was Jehoshaphat's response?

How does this verse bring comfort to you right now? Let the Holy Spirit speak to you.

Memory Verse for Lesson:
If My people who are called by name will humble themselves, and pray and seek my face and turn from their wicked ways, then I will hear from heaven, and will forgive their sin and will heal their land (2 Chronicles 7:14 NKJV).

THE ?ARADOXICAL JESUS in 2 CHRONICLES

We know the Bible does not contradict itself, so it is important to take time to study and understand all sides of the truth and interpret Scripture in light of Scripture to grasp the whole truth as much as possible.

Up through Solomon, God's people enjoyed a United Kingdom, though there were tensions. The split between Israel and Judah was bad news. Issues rose up about where the Temple was placed and Rehoboam did not handle the tension well. Throughout church history we see the Church's fragmentation take its toll. American denominationalism has divided Christians sometimes unnecessarily. Yet Jesus prayed we would all be One (John 17).

Summarize how you live within the church as the institution and yet live as the Body of Christ, a church without walls?

_____
_____
_____
_____

I saw Jesus more clearly in this book when...
_____
_____
_____

JESUS UP CLOSE:

EZRA, NEHEMIAH, AND ESTHER
VIDEO SEGMENT LESSON GUIDE

INTRODUCTION TO *SEEING JESUS* (10-15 MINUTES):
This segment will highlight the books of Ezra, Nehemiah, and Esther. All three contribute a great deal to the history of God's people. Break into groups of two or three and come up with words to describe each of these leaders in the Bible. Share what words came up.

Which words also reflect the character of Jesus?

_____
_____
_____
_____

Watch video segment (approx. 20-30 minutes). Take notes and fill in the blanks.

Brief overview:

1. Northern Kingdom had _____ good kings.

   Captivity to Assyria

2. Southern Kingdom had _____ good kings.

   Josiah last good king

3. Captivity in Babylon (area of Iraq and Iran today) for _____ years.

Two Prophets:

Daniel -

Ezekiel -

Ezra -

Ezra is called by God to lead people back out of captivity.

Cyrus, king of Persia, signs decree.

Isaiah 44:45 – prophesied 100 years before he was born

*See page 133 in study guide

Zerubbabel (descendant of Solomon, ancestor of Joseph) –

Nehemiah –

Israelites stopped building the wall.

4. Nehemiah sees there are _____ gates to Jerusalem.
5. The first thing he built was the _____ .

Nehemiah stands in the gap with prayer.

Nehemiah means: "Comforter."

Fifty-two days:
People rejoiced and encouraged God's people when the wall was completed.

See Page 138 in study guide: Nehemiah's prayer ministry was like the prayer ministry of Jesus.

2 Corinthians 2:14:
"Thanks be to God who always leads us into triumph in Christ and through us diffuses the fragrance of His knowledge in every place" (NKJV).

Sanballot means: "Satan."

ESTHER
Beauty contest: God gives her the most unusual favor.

Haman –

Mordecai –

"If I perish, I perish." — Queen Esther

God's Name hidden: see page 143 in study guide

Esther, which means "star", is a star that points us to Jesus Christ.

Esther means: "Star."

"Stay in the Bible. It is key for us." — Marilyn

Jesus Sightings in Ezra, Nehemiah, Esther (15 minutes):

In studying Ezra, Nehemiah, and Esther, it may be a challenge to see Jesus in the book of Esther without digging a little deeper. Some admirable qualities: Esther was beautiful but used her beauty in the right way; she remained loyal to Mordecai; she had discipline and practiced fasting; she showed shrewdness; and she was a type of savior for her people. To ask to go see the king was dangerous and she knew she could die.

Jesus said we must lay down our life to be a disciple. In what ways has He asked you to die?

What has He asked you to give up?

Share your thoughts on the difference between being a Christian and a disciple.

Wrap Up (10-15 minutes):
In wrapping up the history books, share a time when you encountered Jesus in an unexpected place.

Spend time sharing prayer requests and closing in prayer. Thank Jesus for covering our sin with His victory!

LESSON 15

EZRA: FAITHFUL SCRIBE

In your SEEING JESUS Study Guide:
Read through the fast facts, author and setting, and overview on page 131 and 132. Reflect and take notes.

Jesus in Ezra:

The book of Ezra signifies Christ's work of restoration. Ezra records the Israelites return from captivity under Zerubbabel and under Ezra. The Lord is sovereign over all kingdoms, even pagan rulers. Ezra 3 shows that serving God requires a united effort.

Read Ezra 3:1-13 (NKJV). Circle words and phrases that signal restoration for God's people.

Worship Restored at Jerusalem

And when the seventh month had come, and the children of Israel were in the cities, the people gathered together as one in Jerusalem. **2** Then Jeshua the son of Jozadak and his brethren the priests, and Zerubbabel the son of Shealtiel and his brethren, arose and built the altar of the God of Israel, to sacrifice offer burnt offerings on it, as it is written in the Law of Moses the man of God. **3** Though fear had come upon them because of the people of those countries, they set the altar on its bases; and they offered burnt offerings on it to the Lord, both the morning and evening burnt offerings. **4** They kept the Feast of Tabernacles as it is written, and offered the daily burnt offerings in the number required by ordinance for each day. **5** Afterwards they offered the regular burnt offering, and those for New Moons and for all the appointed feasts of the Lord that were consecrated and those of everyone who willingly offered a freewill offering to the Lord. **6** From the first day of the seventh month they began to offer burnt offerings to the Lord, although the foundation of the temple of the Lord had not been laid. **7** They also gave money to the masons and the carpenters, and food, drink, and oil to the people of Sidon and Tyre to bring cedar logs from Lebanon to the sea, to Joppa, according to the permission which they had from Cyrus king of Persia.

Restoration of the Temple Begins

8 Now in the second month of the second year of their coming to the house of God at Jerusalem, Zerubbabel the son of Shealtiel, Jeshua the son of Jozadak, and the rest of their brethren the priests and the Levites, and all those who had come out of captivity to Jerusalem, began work and appointed the Levites from twenty years old and above to oversee the work of the house of the Lord. **9** Then Jeshua with his sons and brothers Kadmiel with his sons, and the sons of Judah, arose as one to oversee those working on the house of God: the sons of Henadad with their sons and their brethren the Levites.

10 When the builders laid the foundation of the temple of the Lord, the priests stood in their apparel with trumpets, and the Levites the sons of Asaph, with cymbals, to praise the Lord, according to the ordinance of David king of Israel. **11** And they sang responsively, praising and giving thanks to the Lord:

> "For He is good,
>   For His mercy endures forever toward Israel."

Then all the people shouted with a great shout, when they praised the Lord, because the foundation of the house of the Lord was laid.

12 But many of the priests and Levites and heads of the fathers' houses, old men who had seen the first temple, wept with a loud voice when the foundation of this temple was laid before their eyes. Yet many shouted aloud for joy, **13** so that the people could not discern the noise of the shout of joy from the noise of the weeping of the people, shouted with a loud shout, and the sound was heard afar off.

THE NAME EZRA MEANS: **"YAHWEH HELPS"**.

Reflection Exercises:
We read in this passage how the people celebrated the Feast of Tabernacles during the time of rebuilding the altar. This feast was to remember the forty years of wilderness and God's faithfulness. Small huts were built to house travelers en route to worship. God's people had a strong understanding that His presence went with them, no matter if they were in the wilderness or in Zerubbabel's temple. Once again the Israelites could experience the blessing of returning to the Promised Land. How does God show up at this point to show His restorative mercy from Exodus through Ezra?

_____
_____
_____
_____

According to Ezra 3:13, what had come upon the people of God? How did they respond?

What happened in Ezra 3:10 after the foundation was laid?

What is the foundation of the church according to Ephesians 2:19-22?

How did God's people show their trust in God?

Ezra the scribe was a man characterized as: a strong trust in God; moral integrity; and grief over sin.

Unpacking the Outline:
Review page 133 in the study guide.

Ezra 7-10 records the return of God's people under Ezra's leadership as a priest. We can trace his ancestry back to Aaron.

List some words that describe his spiritual ministry among the people.

1. _____
2. _____
3. _____
4. _____
5. _____

From the time the foundation was laid, it took twenty-one years to build the Temple.

Focus: Central Verse / Passage
Ezra's prayer: Ezra 9:8-9

But now, for a brief moment, the Lord our God has been gracious in leaving us a remnant and giving us a firm place in his sanctuary, and so our God gives light to our eyes and a little relief in our bondage. **9** He has shown us kindness in the sight of the kings of Persia: He has granted us new life to rebuild the house of our God and repair its ruins, and he has given us a wall of protection in Judah and Jerusalem.

Though God's people time and time again, fell away from His law, God restored them. Think about a time when you truly fell on the mercy and restorative power of Jesus Christ.

Ezra was an intercessor for God's people. What intercessors has God given you in times you needed someone to go before God on your behalf?

_____
_____
_____
_____
_____

Memory Verse for Lesson:

And they sang responsively, praising and giving thanks to the Lord: "For He is good, For His mercy endures forever toward Israel." Then all the people shouted with a great shout, when they praised the LORD, because the foundation of the house of the Lord was laid (Ezra 3:11 NKJV).

THE ?ARADOXICAL JESUS in EZRA

We know the Bible does not contradict itself, so it is important to take time to study and understand all sides of the truth and interpret Scripture in light of Scripture to grasp the whole truth as much as possible.

A good reminder is that discrepancies we find in the Bible, to the skeptic, will be a contradiction. For Christians, it should be an invitation to explore the text to gain greater understanding. A paradox is not a contraction, rather it is a two truths that seem to contradict.

The number of people, 42,360, are recorded as those returning from Babylon is recorded both in Nehemiah and Ezra. But when you total the lists mentioned in both books, there appears to be a discrepancy in the breakdown of lists of people. Do some research in how these numbers are rectified according to Bible scholars. Explain your findings below:

I saw Jesus more clearly in this book when...

JESUS UP CLOSE:

LESSON 16

NEHEMIAH: RESTORER & REBUILDER

In your SEEING JESUS Study Guide:
Read through the fast facts, author and setting, and overview on page 135 and 136. Reflect and take notes.

Jesus in Nehemiah:

God uses His leaders in different ways to bring about His plan. Many times God uses just one faithful, praying man. We see clearly Nehemiah's humility before God in the beginning of the book.

Read Nehemiah's Prayer (Nehemiah 1:1-11).
Circle words or phrases that show Nehemiah's Christ-like heart as a restorer of God's people:

The words of Nehemiah son of Hakaliah:
In the month of Kislev in the twentieth year, while I was in the citadel of Susa, **2** Hanani, one of my brothers, came from Judah with some other men, and I questioned them about the Jewish remnant that had survived the exile, and also about Jerusalem.

3 They said to me, "Those who survived the exile and are back in the province are in great trouble and disgrace. The wall of Jerusalem is broken down, and its gates have been burned with fire."

4 When I heard these things, I sat down and wept. For some days I mourned and fasted and prayed before the God of heaven.

5 Then I said:
"Lord, the God of heaven, the great and awesome God, who keeps his covenant of love with those who love him and keep his commandments, **6** let your ear be attentive and your eyes open to hear the prayer your servant is praying before you day and night for your servants, the people of Israel. I confess the sins we Israelites, including myself and my father's family, have committed against you. **7** We have acted very wickedly toward you. We have not obeyed the commands, decrees and laws you gave your servant Moses.

8 "Remember the instruction you gave your servant Moses, saying, 'If you are unfaithful, I will scatter you among the nations, **9** but if you return to me and obey my commands, then even if your exiled people are at the farthest horizon, I will gather them from there and bring them to the place I have chosen as a dwelling for my Name.'

10 "They are your servants and your people, whom you redeemed by your great strength and your mighty hand. **11** Lord, let your ear be attentive to the prayer of this your servant and to the prayer of your servants who delight in revering your name. Give your servant success today by granting him favor in the presence of this man."
I was cupbearer to the king.

Reflection Exercises:
What was Nehemiah's first reaction when hearing the trouble the Jewish remnant were facing?

Read verse 6. What was his prayer here?

Though all of our sins are forgiven, both confessed and unconfessed, why is it important to confess our sins before God?

Nehemiah exemplified a powerful prayer life, just as Jesus showed His disciples. Prayer requires humble submission to God. When do you find it most difficult to submit your will to God?

_____
_____
_____
_____
_____
_____

> *GIVE YOUR SERVANT SUCCESS TODAY BY GRANTING HIM FAVOR.*
> *— NEHEMIAH 1:11*

Unpacking the Outline:
Review the chart on page 138 of the study guide.
Under Nehemiah's leadership everything was restored, except for a king. The next king would be the Messiah.

There are nine different prayers recorded in Nehemiah to show the breadth of his prayers. He makes a point to even pray for his enemies, which is something Jesus also asked us to do. He often waited on God showing sensitivity to His leading. Think about a time when you waited on God and saw Him do more than you could have on your own?

As you read through the outline, list some of the roles of Nehemiah. Write out some phrases that describe his leadership.

_____
_____
_____
_____
_____
_____

Focus: Central Verse / Passage

> *I AM CARRYING ON A GREAT PROJECT AND CANNOT GO DOWN. WHY SHOULD THE WORK STOP WHILE I LEAVE IT AND GO DOWN TO YOU? — NEHEMIAH 6:3*

Nehemiah's response seems like a haughty reply but he correctly discerned the insincerity of his enemies. Conflict is often the way leaders become side tracked from what God is calling them to do. List some of the oppositions you have faced when you felt called to a specific task the Lord gave you.

How did God prove faithful in the time of opposition?

Nehemiah's administration teaches us that God alone is the one to be feared, not our enemy.

Memory Verse for Lesson:
Now therefore, O God, strengthen my hands (Nehemiah 6:9b NKJV).

THE ?ARADOXICAL JESUS in NEHEMIAH

We know the Bible does not contradict itself, so it is important we take time to study and understand all sides of the truth and interpret Scripture in light of Scripture to understand.

Reread the following verse: Nehemiah 9:32-37
Confessing sin publically isn't something the church is accustomed to today. In the book of Nehemiah, we see God's people take responsibility for their sin corporately and individually.

How can confession become legalistic?

How can it make us more grace-conscious?

_____
_____
_____
_____
_____
_____

Read what Jesus warns against in Matthew 6:5-8. Does this contradict how the Israelites confessed? Explain why or why not.

_____
_____
_____
_____
_____
_____

I saw Jesus more clearly in this book when...

_____
_____
_____

JESUS UP CLOSE:

LESSON 17

ESTHER: INTERCESSOR

In your SEEING JESUS Study Guide:
Read through the fast facts, author and setting, and overview on page 141 and 142. Reflect and take notes.

Jesus in Esther:

Queen Esther was used strategically to save her people. Because of her willingness to stand in the gap, a Holocaust was avoided. The entire narrative takes place in Persia. Esther is the second book named after a woman. Though there is no direct mention of God, it seems the author used it to only highlight how God uses a plot, people, and circumstances to bring about His will, whether He is recognized or not. Clearly, Esther was a mediator, just as Christ was our mediator.

Read Esther 4:1-16 NKJV
Circle any words or phrases that reveal Esther as a type of Christ for her people:

When Mordecai learned all that had happened, he tore his clothes and put on sackcloth and ashes, and went out into the midst of the city. He cried out with a loud and bitter cry. **2** He went as far as the front of the king's gate, for no one might enter the king's gate clothed with sackcloth. **3** And in every province where the king's command and decree arrived, there was great mourning among the Jews, with fasting, weeping, and wailing; and many lay in sackcloth and ashes.

4 So Esther's maids and eunuchs came and told her, and the queen was deeply distressed. Then she sent garments to clothe Mordecai and take his sackcloth away from him, but he would not accept them. **5** Then Esther called

Hathach, one of the king's eunuchs whom he had appointed to attend her, and she gave him a command concerning Mordecai, to learn what and why this was. **6** So Hathach went out to Mordecai in the city square that was in front of the king's gate. **7** And Mordecai told him all that had happened to him, and the sum of money that Haman had promised to pay into the king's treasuries to destroy the Jews. **8** He also gave him a copy of the written decree for their destruction, which was given at Shushan, that he might show it to Esther and explain it to her, and that he might command her to go in to the king to make supplication to him and plead before him for her people. **9** So Hathach returned and told Esther the words of Mordecai.

10 Then Esther spoke to Hathach, and gave him a command for Mordecai: **11** "All the king's servants and the people of the king's provinces know that any man or woman who goes into the inner court to the king, who has not been called, he has but one law: put all to death, except the one to whom the king holds out the golden scepter, that he may live. Yet I myself have not been called to go in to the king these thirty days." **12** So they told Mordecai Esther's words.

13 And Mordecai told them to answer Esther: "Do not think in your heart that you will escape in the king's palace any more than all the other Jews. **14** For if you remain completely silent at this time, relief and deliverance will arise for the Jews from another place, but you and your father's house will perish. Yet who knows whether you have come to the kingdom for such a time as this?"

15 Then Esther told them to reply to Mordecai:
16 "Go, gather together all the Jews who are in Susa, and fast for me. Do not eat or drink for three days, night or day. I and my attendants will fast as you do. When this is done, I will go to the king, even though it is against the law. And if I perish, I perish."

Reflection Exercises:
How did Mordecai's response impact Esther?

In what ways can we see Esther was not blinded by materialism, though living in the palace?

To see humanity in intense pain, is difficult. Think of a time you saw someone weep bitterly, as described in Esther. How did Jesus respond to the pain of others?

___
___
___
___
___

The book of Esther chronologically fits in between the sixth and seventh chapters of Ezra.

Unpacking the Outline:
See page 144 in your study guide.

Review Esther 1-2.

The book of Esther largely deals with the theme of God's providence. Write out a short list of how God used circumstances to lead Esther to the king's palace:

1. ___
2. ___
3. ___
4. ___
5. ___

What impact did Mordecai have in the book of Esther?

___
___
___
___
___

> "GO, GATHER TOGETHER ALL THE JEWS WHO ARE IN SUSA, AND FAST FOR ME. DO NOT EAT OR DRINK FOR THREE DAYS, NIGHT OR DAY. I AND MY ATTENDANTS WILL FAST AS YOU DO. WHEN THIS IS DONE, I WILL GO TO THE KING, EVEN THOUGH IT IS AGAINST THE LAW. AND IF I PERISH, I PERISH. — **ESTHER 4:16**"

How has God used people in your life to change the course of your plans for the better?

_____
_____
_____
_____
_____

Write out a short paragraph about someone who pointed you in the right direction when you needed wisdom.

_____
_____
_____
_____
_____

God's Providence in the Book of Esther:

1. Mordecai's honor recorded in the palace records
2. Esther's admission to the king's court
3. God guides the timing of the two feasts
4. Haman's gallows end up hanging Haman

Focus: Central Verse / Passage in Esther

Without the book of Esther, we would not know the origin of the Feast of Purim, which marked the deliverance of God's people from the hands of the enemy. Purim is a celebration of joyful rest. God's people survived the threat of death:

"For the Jews it was a time of happiness and joy, gladness and honor" (Esther 8:16).

"This happened on the thirteenth day of the month of Adar, and on the fourteenth they rested and made it a day of feasting and joy" (Esther 9:17).

*The word **"Purim"** is the plural form of the Hebrew word **"Pur"** which means "Lots" or "Fate". Haman had "cast lots" to determine a day to exterminate God's People throughout the Persian Empire.*

Purim is a kind of Sabbath. What are some reasons that observing a day of joyful rest is a healthy practice?

_____
_____
_____
_____
_____

How has Jesus allowed us to rest from our enemies?

_____
_____
_____
_____
_____

> *THE JEWS DID NOT COMMEMORATE THE DAY OF THEIR VICTORIOUS BATTLE, BUT THE DAY ON WHICH THEY RESTED FROM THEIR ENEMIES.*
> **— ADELE BERLIN, JEWISH COMMENTATOR**

List some situations in your own life that you would like to experience God's rest:

_____
_____
_____
_____
_____

Memory verse for lesson:
For if you remain completely silent at this time, relief and deliverance will arise for the Jews from another place, but you and your father's house will perish. Yet who knows whether you have come to the kingdom for such a time as this? (Esther 4:14 NKJV).

THE ?ARADOXICAL JESUS in ESTHER

We know the Bible does not contradict itself, so it is important we take time to study and understand all sides of the truth and interpret Scripture in light of Scripture to understand.

Some problems associated with the book of Esther: the lack of a single mention of God; and the moral practices of Mordecai and Esther in the deliverance process.

A question to help with these tensions is to remember the immorality of God's people throughout the pre-exilic period. How does God still rule perfectly through the rule of imperfect people?

What are some reasons a clear reference to God is not mentioned?

What can God's silence communicate? What happens when we conduct our own affairs without consulting God?

I saw Jesus more clearly in this book when...

JESUS UP CLOSE:

NOTES

NOTES

NOTES

APPENDEX
LEADER'S GUIDE & ANSWER KEYS

LEADER'S GUIDE: INTRODUCTION

I'm so glad you decided to make the commitment to take a deeper look at Scripture using the *Seeing Jesus Bible Encounter Series Workbook*. Throughout my years of teaching the Bible, I find one of the most encouraging encounters we can have is to see Jesus, the Living Word, in the most surprising and unexpected places. Jesus Christ, the cornerstone of our faith, is the One we are to imitate and follow. Through this study, I know you will be encouraged by the power of the Word and actively see Jesus through the pages of both the Old and New Testament.

I want to warmly welcome you, dear friend, and leader of the group. I wish there was a way I could sit in on your study group and hear the stories around the table. In this volume, I know you will encounter many unexpected blessings that only Jesus can give you. You will have the opportunity to hear some of the insights from Scripture that God has revealed to me, and those you are studying with, and together, we will also see Jesus much more clearly. I'm very excited about this resource that supplements my, *Seeing Jesus Bible Encounter Study Guide*. The workbook and the study guide work well together and will reinforce your study. You may choose to do this as an independent learner or in a small group or church learning environment.

VOLUME 1 : LEADER'S GUIDE

The *Seeing Jesus Bible Encounter Series Workbooks* contain the following study material:

1. THE PENTATEUCH – VOLUME 1
2. HISTORY – VOLUME 2
3. POETRY / WISDOM BOOKS – VOLUME 3
4. MAJOR / MINOR PROPHETS – VOLUME 4
5. GOSPELS / ACTS & ROMANS – VOLUME 5
6. EPISTLES – VOLUME 6
7. END TIMES – VOLUME 7

You'll be amazed at the Jesus sightings we found throughout every volume. And our encounters with Jesus, I know, He will meet your you right where you are, as He is the Bread of Life. My prayer is this will move well past head knowledge to the heart, where faith can be lived out. With that, let's take a look at the format. Whether you are leading the group or leading yourself through this study, this will help acclimate you to the materials and be prepared to receive as much as you can as you look at each book of the Bible.

Study Format

The lessons will give you a key concept for each book to help you remember the focus of the book. The following sections are consistent throughout each volume, which include reflection exercises, scripture reading, memorization exercises, and practical application steps.

1. Jesus in (respective book name here)
2. Unpacking the Outline
3. Focus: Central Passage
4. Memory Verse for Lesson
5. Paradoxical Jesus
6. Jesus Up Close

These lessons are set up to work well in a 60-90 minute session, depending on the size of your group. Through these sections, you will have various opportunities to grab hold of the context and see where Jesus shows up. Don't rush! Enjoy these moments in the Word and invite Him to show you deep revelations that you could not grasp without the help of His Spirit (Jeremiah 33:3).

Group Study—Lesson 1
Your weekly group gathering will take around one and a half hours to complete. This will be a good length to plan for when you are using the study guide or engaging in the video lessons. The weeks when a video lesson applies, note that the video length is about **20 minutes**. Allow time for discussion and prayer.

Video
When there is a video lesson, use it as main focus for the study group. Summary points with fill-in-the-blank questions and some key concepts are included for you to complete as you follow along with the video.

Small Group Discussion
Following the video, you'll see a section of small group discussion questions. Let these questions guide you as you discuss God's promises with fellow believers. Learn from those who have been given different experiences with God's promises. Refer to the leader's guide for further supplemental material listed in subsequent pages.

Prayer
The group discussion time each week will conclude with a time of prayer. Through this study, I want to stress the importance of prayer as our lifeline to God's grace. Some participants in your group may be new to this type of setting, so be sensitive to where the comfort level of praying out loud might be. As a facilitator/leader, take the lead in making sure everyone is prayed for each week.

Start Up
As you have read over the introduction, I want to take a moment to specifically encourage you as one who will create an inviting environment for all the participants. I pray God uses your gifts to help facilitate this study. It is important for you to feel comfortable with the format and style so that you can answer questions and provide support as needed. While your responsibilities are mainly fulfilled in guiding everyone through the sections each time you meet, you may also want to make yourself available to participants throughout the week, whether it is for prayer support or direction in understanding the Scriptures.

Resources Needed
You will need a **DVD player** and a **room or facility** that is conducive to small group discussions. You may want to bring **extra Bibles** for those who may not have one or forget theirs. You may also wish to bring several translations of the Bible to the study. Encourage participants to raise questions and find answers together. Make a point to make everyone feel comfortable, connected, and allow participants the opportunity to share their insights when appropriate.

Prior to each session, take time to review your leader's guide to help focus your preparation for the coming lessons. You will find additional discussion questions and bonus information that may help create more interaction. I would encourage you to watch the video lesson segments prior to facilitating to sharpen your grasp of the material and as a way to prepare for the discussions.

Study Group Dynamics
Because of the types of study and reflection questions, I'd recommend that your breakout groups be no larger than three to five participants. This will offer some level of intimacy and the ability to answer any questions in greater depth. This will also cultivate a prayerful learning environment. You may want to monitor group discussions from a distance to assure participants feel comfortable in their groups. Encourage everyone to be open as they share answers to the discussion questions, but also not to be afraid of silence or giving a wrong answer. There are no wrong answers in group discussions and all are qualified to answer, whether the participant is a new believer or a seasoned Christian.

Leader's Role
I encourage you to be prepared with the weekly lesson prior to your day of study together. Read over the sections and fill in answers ahead of time. Reading the highlighted passages ahead of time will be a great way to anticipate questions and lead with more confidence. However, you do not have to speak through every part of the lesson. Avoid dominating the discussion with your own insights. Most of the deeper teaching moments will come from the group's reflections collectively.

Time Keeping
It will be up to you to move the groups along and keep things close to the suggested time allotment noted beside each lesson. Be respectful of schedules, offering closure at the time agreed upon so no one feels left out of prayer time at the end of each lesson.

For the first lesson, take a bit of time to introduce yourself. Share how you learned about the *Seeing Jesus* resource and what led you to host the group. Make sure everyone has a chance to become acquainted. You may have committed to studying all seven volumes, or perhaps just one volume. The study works well to add participants at any time, so welcome those who may join later. It is a study where anyone could easily begin at any week and finish missed sessions independently.

Video Segment
When it applies, make sure the technical equipment is set up in plenty of time so you can begin the DVD once everyone is ready. Some participants may miss the fill-in-the-blank answers, so point others to the answers supplied in the back of the study guide.

I'd encourage you to solicit feedback after the first session to make sure the setting met the needs of your participants.

ADDITIONAL STUDY NOTES

VOLUME 2 – HISTORY

LESSON 6 : JOSHUA

Warm-up exercise:
When we think of Joshua, courage often comes to mind. In what ways did Joshua show his courage came from God? Now think about a modern day hero. Who is a modern day hero of yours? Share and discuss.

>> *Fact: Joshua was born a slave in Egypt but became a leader in Canaan. He led Israel for 25 years and died at 110 years of age.*

In Hebrew, the understanding of a name is tied to "fragrance". The name "Joshua" is the equivalent of the New Testament name, "Jesus."

Bonus Question:
Joshua's great challenge to us is found in Joshua 24:15, "Choose this day whom you will serve." How is God asking you to serve Him in a way that requires supernatural courage?

LESSON 7 – JUDGES

Warm-up exercise:
Judges is a book about sin and its consequences. Discuss the definition of "sin" as a group. The Christian doctrine about sin often offends nonbelievers as we continue to hear, "everyone is inherently good." Share how grace has freed you from living under the shame of sin. Close the discussion with statements of gratitude about His restoring power

>> *Fact: The cycles of sin are repeated in the book of Judges: rebellion, retribution, repentance, restoration, and rest. Does this translate to the church today? Discuss.*

Group Exercise:
Pair up and assign each group to look at two or three judges up close. Add more accordingly until all judges are covered. Give each group about 10 minutes to research their assigned judges. Then have each group share the insights, facts, learned about each judge.

Bonus Question:
What was Israel's primary source of failure during the period of the Judges?

LESSON 8 – RUTH

Warm-up Exercise:
We've all heard mother-in-law jokes. But in Ruth, we see a friendship and loyalty between Naomi and Ruth that rises above our cultural understanding. Share as a group the blessing of family through marriage and how it has blessed your heritage of faith.

Meaning and names in the book of Ruth:

Ruth – friendship
Naomi – pleasant
Mara – bitter
Boaz – In His strength
Bethlehem – House of bread
Elimelech – My God is King

Bonus question:
Ruth shows the redemptive power of loyalty to God and loyalty to family. Think about a family member who is far from the Lord. How does a household of faith offer protection to family members not yet saved?

LESSON 9 – 1 SAMUEL

Warm-up exercise:
Samuel begins to discern the voice of God as a boy. Share your experiences in learning to hear the voice of God. Discuss how the Lord speaks to you personally and in what ways you want to hear him better?

>> *Fact: Samuel was born around 1105 B.C.*

Bonus question:
Samuel began the school of prophets. How does OT and NT prophesy differ from your understanding of Scripture? What are some ways we can recognize false prophets today?

Overview:
Samuel provides the background of transition from:

Eli to Samuel

Samuel to Saul

Saul to David

LESSON 10 – 2 SAMUEL

Warm-up exercise:
David's life is the central theme of 2 Samuel. Brainstorm words that describe King David, both positive and negative. Have someone in your group write them down on a white board or large piece of paper. Discuss the list and how God used both his strengths and weaknesses.

Interesting fact:
David chronologically is halfway between Abraham and Jesus Christ.

Bonus Group activity:
King David made a lasting mark on culture and the Christian faith. What contemporary leader can you think of who has done something similar in marking the world with the Kingdom of God. (i.e. Dietrich Bonhoeffer, CS Lewis, William Wilberforce). Share your insights on what makes them unique to other world leaders.

Bonus Question:
Unlike the kings to follow, David did not allow idolatry to come between him and God, though he did struggle with personal sin. Why do you think this is true of David?

David's reign: 7 1/2 years over Judah; 33 years over Judah and Israel

LESSON 11 – 1 KINGS

Warm-up exercise:
Have each person in your group share one new fact or insight they learned about their faith from studying the history books so far.

> >> *Fact: 1 Kings covers a span of about 120 years, beginning with the reign of King Solomon, David's and Bathsheba's son.*

Bonus Question:
David's sin caused him a great deal of sorrow. When someone sins against God as a leader, the consequences also impact the followers or a community. How can you trace David's sin in Solomon's reign? In what ways have you seen Christians handle the restoration process well? What are some wrong ways you've seen leadership handle public sin?

Four major events recorded:

David's death

Solomon's reign

The Kingdom divided

Elijah's ministry

LESSON 12 – 2 KINGS

Warm-up exercises:
The drama of the divided kingdom continues in 2 Kings. What insights have you gained in your study of the different dynasties? Why do you think the Northern kingdom produced more wicked kings than the South? Share your theories as a group.

>> *Fact: Israel's united kingdom lasted 120 years. Total kingdom period lasted a total of 467 years.*

Prophets in Northern Kingdom:
Elijah, Elisha, Hosea, and Amos

Prophets of the Southern Kingdom:
Isaiah, Obadiah, Micah, Jeremiah, Nahum, Zephaniah, Habakkuk.

Bonus Activity:
Study the prophetic ministry of Elisha and compare his words and warnings to what we have in Hosea or Amos. Discuss your insights as a group.

LESSON 13 – 1 CHRONICLES

Warm-up exercise:
Put some names, in a hat or small bowl, of the prophets and kings studied so far. Write a quote or deed they did on the front side of the paper and read aloud. (Example: I was a prophet of the Northern Kingdom who asked for a double portion. Who am I? Answer. Elisha)

>> *Fact: Genealogies from Adam to David are recorded in the first nine chapters. These chapters provided one of the most extensive table of records in the Bible.*

Bonus Question:
David's desire to the build the temple is stressed in 1 Chronicles. David's heart for worship gave him great intimacy with God. How can we cultivate stronger hearts for worship beyond church walls?

LESSON 14- 2 CHRONICLES

Warm-up exercise:
Compare and contrast David's reign with his son Solomon's. How can we see similar characteristics? Successes and failures? Think about a mentor in your life. What is one of the most valuable things you've learned from them?

Legendary things about Solomon's reign:
His wealth, wisdom, the temple, his palace.

Bonus Activity:
Amon is said to be the worst, most wicked of kings and Josiah one of the best. Amon's reign lasted two years; Josiah's reign lasted 31. Study a bit about these two kings and compare and contrast your findings.

LESSON 15 – EZRA

Warm-up lesson:
A remnant of God's people return from Babylon in Ezra. Think of a time when you felt like you were in "captivity." How did God bring you out of it?

Ezra was a contemporary of Nehemiah; a scribe

> >> Fact: *A remnant returns from Babylonian captivity after 70 years—called Israel's second Exodus.*

Tribes who returned:
Judah, Benjamin, and Levi

> >> Fact: *Between chapters 6 and 7 is when Esther lived.*

Characteristics of Ezra:
  A strong trust in God
  Moral integrity
  Grief over sin

LESSON 16 - NEHEMIAH

Warm-up exercise:
Often God raises up one man at a key time to do something remarkable that impacts a whole nation. Nehemiah knew how to stay focused on the task and shepherd the people. He prayed for God's forgiveness and for God's mercy to help him rebuild the wall. One of his most striking strengths was his recourse to pray. Take time to skim through his prayers in the first chapters of the book to see how he dealt with opposition. Share your reflections with one another.

Bonus Question:
Nehemiah was governor of Jerusalem for 14 years. Do you think it is possible to be an honest politician today?

> >> Fact: *The walls of Jerusalem had been destroyed.*
> >> Fact: *Malachi ministers as a contemporary of Nehemiah.*

Group activity:
The wall was finished in 52 days. Think about a service project your small group can do that will benefit a group of people or your community. Commit the project to prayer and on the 52nd day, celebrate together what God did to multiply your efforts.

LESSON 17 - ESTHER

Warm-up exercise:
Esther begins with the mention of a beauty pageant. Think about what is stressed in beauty pageants today. Define "beauty" as a group. Compare and contrast similarities in your definition.

> >> Fact: *The name Esther has several meanings: "star"; hidden concealment; Her Jewish name, Hadassah means "myrtle."*

VOLUME 1 : LEADER'S GUIDE

Bonus Question:
The providence of God is stressed over and over again in the book of Esther. What was your last providential moment with God? Esther was given great favor in the sight of the king. When were you given unmerited favor that allowed you to accomplish something to glorify God?

The omission of God's name does not detract from the theological worth of Esther. It could be interpreted as His hiddenness to work out His purposes.

The book of Esther provides the only biblical portrait of the majority of Jews who remained in Persia.

ANSWER KEY

VOLUME 2 – HISTORY

LESSON: JOSHUA
1. History
2. Manna
3. 6 1/2 years
4. Meditate
5. 2 million

LESSON: JUDGES AND RUTH
1. Holy Spirit
2. Spirit-filled
3. Miracles
4. Spirit of the Lord
5. Clothes
6. Philistines
7. Physical Strength
8. Expected, exceptional, extraordinary

LESSON: 1 & 2 SAMUEL
1. Jesus
2. Have children
3. Grace
4. Crisis
5. Lovingkindness

LESSON: KINGS & PROPHETS 1
1. Drought
2. Ahab
3. Ravens
4. Widow

LESSON: KINGS & PROPHETS 2
1. Bathsheba
2. Proverbs, wisdom
3. Wisdom, understanding
4. 500
5. Anointed one

LESSON: KINGS & PROPHETS 3
1. Profitable
2. David
3. Alcoholic

LESSON: EZRA, NEHEMIAH, ESTHER
1. 0
2. 9
3. 7
4. 12
5. Altar